WIRELESS NETWORKING
MADE EASY

WIRELESS NETWORKING MADE EASY

Everything You Need to Know to Build Your Own PANs, LANs, and WANs

Russell Shaw

AMACOM

American Management Association

New York • Atlanta • Brussels • Chicago • Mexico City • San Francisco
Shanghai • Tokyo • Toronto • Washington, D.C.

Special discounts on bulk quantities of AMACOM books are available to corporations, professional associations, and other organizations. For details, contact Special Sales Department, AMACOM, a division of American Management Association, 1601 Broadway, New York, NY 10019.
Tel.: 212-903-8316. Fax: 212-903-8083.
Web site: www.amacombooks.org

This publication is designed to provide accurate and authoritative information in regard to the subject matter covered. It is sold with the understanding that the publisher is not engaged in rendering legal, accounting, or other professional service. If legal advice or other expert assistance is required, the services of a competent professional person should be sought.

Shaw, Russell, 1947-
    Wireless networking made easy: everything you need to know to
       build your own PANs, LANs, and WANs / Russell Shaw.
         p. cm.
    ISBN 0-8144-7175-7 (pbk.)
    1. Wireless local area networks—Amateurs' manuals. 2. Wide area
networks—Amateurs' manuals. I. Title
TK5105.78.S525 2003
004.67—dc21   2003006177

Printing number
10 9 8 7 6 5 4 3 2 1

DEDICATION

I would like to dedicate this book to my love, Mary. Not only does she walk with me through this world, but we have been communicating "wirelessly," over short and long distances, ever since we met.

CONTENTS

PREFACE

Wireless Networking Made Easy will provide you with an overview of wireless technologies with a focus on how devices and applications work together to increase productivity in personal area networks (PANs), local area networks (LANs), and wide area networks (WANs).

In this book, you will learn how to identify business problems that are candidates for wireless solutions, how to choose the appropriate wireless solution, and through examples, what it takes to implement that solution. The book also includes a technical overview of the standards and systems behind wireless technologies.

After you finish this book, you will have a good, basic knowledge of what wireless networking is and how you can use it to increase your productivity in any size network.

This book is divided into fifteen chapters, the first of which provides an overview of wireless networking and devices and addresses common questions and concerns about wireless. You will then learn about three wireless solutions: PANs, LANs, and WANs. You will learn how to identify which solution is best suited for your company, your office, or your home, and then you will learn more about each of these solutions.

TEN REASONS WHY YOU NEED A WIRELESS NETWORK

If you are unsure whether you even need a wireless network, let me try to convince you that a wireless network may well be the ideal communications solution for your business, your home, or both.

When it comes to specific technology and communications solutions, every business and home has slightly different needs. Your requirements will vary depending on the nature of your business, the size of your network, the suitability of your office building or home to accommodate wireless upgrades, the flexibility of your budget, as well as the types of information you wish to send over your wireless (or wired) connection.

Here are some commonly applicable reasons why you should consider a wireless network:

1. Wireless networks can be simply installed, used, and quickly expanded as your communications needs evolve.

2. Wireless LANs and PANs save you from dealing with the confusing clutter of wires, cables, and connections inherent in most wired networks.

3. If your business is located in an older building with a limited capacity to accept a wired networking upgrade, a wireless network might be an ideal solution. That is because in wireless networks, the communications technology is largely contained in the specific equipment, rather than through costly, power-draining wired connections.

4. Wireless networks can be configured to provide Internet access in conference rooms where a standard Internet connection is not likely to have been installed. This function enables you to conduct training sessions and sales presentations that use Internet- or Intranet-based resources.

5. If you are remodeling your office, wireless networking allows you to handle the transition without expensive recabling work necessary to disconnect your desktop computer and peripheral equipment such as scanners and printers. If you have a wireless network already in operation, all you will need to do is plug in your desktop computer at your new desk.

6. Wireless networks offer a comparatively quick return on investment. A 2002 study by the Wireless LAN Association found that the average time to pay back the initial costs of WLAN installations in full was 8.9 months.

7. If your workforce is equipped with Wi-Fi–enabled notebook computers, they will be able to access corporate information as well as their own E-Mail without having to search for a phone connection to plug their computer into.

8. Devices connected by Bluetooth over a wireless PAN can share resources. For example, your mobile phone, personal digital assistant (PDA), and personal computer may be able to share the same address book, to-do list, and schedule.

9. If you want to connect your Bluetooth-enabled devices, you will not have to go through the hassle of using a sync cradle with accompanying software. As just one example, your PDA will automatically synchronize with your personal computer when you arrive in your office.

10. When wireless LANs are bridged, creating a wireless WAN, users in different locations can access the Internet, share files, and access network resources without wires. These networks are especially prevalent in the health care and education sectors, where operations may be simultaneously taking place on large campuses with geographically separated facilities.

ACKNOWLEDGMENTS

Thanks to Jacquie Flynn at AMACOM Books for envisioning this project when others thought it would sell only to geeks and IT folks. I am also grateful to the many able hands at AMACOM and Maryland Composition, for bringing this book to life. And finally, kudos to my agent, Carole McClendon of Waterside Productions. When an honest and extremely able go-getter believes in you and the quality of your work, it is yet another occasion to feel blessed.

WIRELESS NETWORKING MADE EASY

UNDERSTANDING THE WIRELESS WORLD

Networking is a technology that enables two or more computers to be linked together. The purpose of doing so is so that they can communicate as well as share resources such as printers, scanners, files, CD-ROM drives, Internet access, spreadsheets and accounting packages, and other specialized software.

THE WIRELESS COMPUTING ENVIRONMENT

Wireless networking technology is not difficult to install at your business or even your home. You do not need to be a technical genius to install and operate a computer network. More importantly, the long-term benefits alleviate any fears you may have that your computers will be unavailable for the short period it takes to configure your network.

In a wireless network, all of the computers broadcast their information to one another using radio signals. This can make networking extremely easy, especially if you have computers all over your office

Figure 1-1. This notebook computer has a wireless network card.

or home. It also makes it much easier to move computers around. For example, a laptop with a wireless network card would be completely portable throughout your office (see Figure 1-1).

Wires may suggest a busy office full of the latest equipment, but wires can actually be an inefficient networking medium. Additionally, wires detract from the aesthetic appearance of your computing setup.

Imagine your computers and communication devices tied together without wires. A wireless network will give you increased mobility and allow you to share files, printers, other computing devices, and Internet access without wires.

AN OVERVIEW OF WIRELESS NETWORKING

You have a choice of three technologies when it comes to wireless networking for your office or home. Which one you choose to implement will largely be based on your computing needs, as well as the type of computing and communications equipment you have available to network.

The three basic wireless networking technologies you may wish to consider include wireless private area networks (PANs), wireless wide area networks (WANs), and wireless local area networks (LANs).

A PAN refers to a confined short-range network. For instance, all the devices connected within your cubicle would be your PAN. Another example of a PAN would be all the devices you carry with you while you travel (i.e., your notebook computer, personal digital assistant [PDA], cell phone, etc.).

A relatively new concept, a PAN is an ad hoc network created by Bluetooth-enabled devices. (Bluetooth is named after Harald Bluetooth, who was king of Denmark between 940 and 981 and who united Denmark and Norway.)

Bluetooth is a short-range cable replacement technology for linking digital consumer electronic devices. Bluetooth provides a mechanism for forming small wireless networks of Bluetooth-equipped products, equipped with antennas for communicating with the PAN (see Figure 1-2). It enables users to connect a wide range of computing and telecommunications devices easily and simply without having to buy, carry, or connect cables. The technology can also replace multiple cable connections via a single radio link.

All that is needed to create a PAN is to walk into a room with a Bluetooth-compliant device and it will connect with other Bluetooth devices in the room. This simplicity makes Bluetooth suitable for users who are not "techies" but who need to hook up their computers or devices easily.

A wireless LAN consists of two main components: an access point and a wireless LAN card. The wireless LAN card will be a PC card for

Figure 1-2. These devices are all Bluetooth-enabled.

a notebook computer, or PC card and a PCI (Peripheral Component Interconnect) adapter or a Universal Serial Bus (USB) device for your desktop computer. A peripheral bus commonly used in PCs, Macintoshes and PCI adapters, incidentally, provides a path for data to travel at high speeds between the computer's Central Processing Unit and peripheral devices used by the computer

The access point is a bridge between your wired network and your wireless network (see Figure 1-3). The access point then allows your wireless LAN card to communicate with your wired network, giving you the ability to walk around the office campus and access whatever is on your LAN (E-Mail, Internet, files) as long as you are within proximity of the access point. In the case of a desktop PC, a wireless LAN enables you to get network access into conference rooms or hard-to-wire areas. To set up files and print shared information within an office is as easy as with a wired LAN. An alternative to the traditional access point for a small network is the PCI card. If you already have a desktop PC and adequate software, you can plug a PCI card into it and essentially use the PC as your access point.

A WAN is a computer data network with computers connected over long distances. A wireless WAN uses radio signals to receive and transmit data using radio signals over the initial interconnect with the

Figure 1-3. The Access Point forms a bridge between a wired and wireless network.

mobile computer system. At the central connection points, the segments of the wireless WAN connect to each other via telephone or other high-speed communications links.

IS WIRELESS NETWORKING RIGHT FOR YOU?

There are pros and cons to both wired and wireless networks. Every business communications situation has its own unique requirements.

To make a decision about networking technology for your business, you will need to go through a two-step process. First, evaluate your current general networking capabilities. Second, consider your future networking needs. It is likely that a wireless network of one type or another will present a valuable solution, perhaps even relieve technical communications obstacles you never even knew you had.

In assessing your networking capabilities, some of the factors you should take into consideration include:

✔ What, if any, is your current networking technology?

✔ Is your workplace wired with Category 5 cabling? This cabling is required for fast Ethernet access, a necessity for an in-office wired network.

✔ How many people use the computers and communications systems in your company now?

✔ Do you conduct business at locations away from your primary work area? A key example would be a conference room setting, where your notebook PCs need to connect to your office computing network.

✔ Another scenario would be if you take your notebook computers to one of your coworkers' desks or offices, and tried to hook up to your network from there.

✔ In your office, what is the proportion of notebook to desktop PCs currently in use?

If you have a well-established, fairly large office already wired with a network connected to only desktop PCs, and do not expect too much growth in the future, you may not need a wireless network. However, this does not take into account that virtually all businesses operate with notebook computers, portable communications devices, and desktop PCs that should all fit together.

WIRELESS NETWORKS HAVE WIRED NETWORKS BEAT

A wireless network has several major advantages over a wired network. Some of these advantages are:

✔ Ease of installation. It can be expensive to wire your building with Category 5 cabling to enable Ethernet capability. Even if you can afford it, the existing utility capacity of your building may not easily allow for it, and your landlord may not welcome it.

✔ Flexibility. If you plan to be expanding or moving offices or even rearranging an existing office, wireless networks provide a short transition period. The ease-of-installation wireless networks offer should allay any fears on your part that your business will suffer burdensome and lengthy interruptions while you upgrade.

✔ Convenient information access. The most exciting advantage you will realize with wireless networking will be your ability to have access to your information through your notebook computer even when you are not at your LAN connection. Do members of your staff travel frequently, and need this connection? Do some occasionally telecommute from home? By offering your employees access to information in an easy and speedy way, wireless networking will considerably enhance the productivity of your business.

Wireless Networks: A Fast and Inexpensive Future

As newer technology enables your computers to communicate with each other at faster speeds than are now possible, wireless networking will become more common. Because more equipment necessary for the performance of wireless networks will be manufactured, the economics of scale will lower the price of configuring a wireless network.

Within the next year, wireless networks will be operating at speeds three to four times greater than now. As information access becomes ubiquitous, the productivity of your staff will continue to increase at a rapid rate.

QUESTIONS AND CONCERNS ABOUT WIRELESS

With any new technology—including wireless networking—concerns and questions arise. These concerns and questions, including safety, security, cost, and interoperability, are addressed here.

Safety

Much has been written in the media about the health risks of exposure to radiofrequency electromagnetic energy. Manufacturers of wireless networking devices are required to design their products to conform to exposure guidelines set forth by various standards organizations. These organizations, such as the prestigious Institute of Electrical and Electronic Engineers (IEEE), continue to monitor and conduct research into the levels and types of radio transmission considered safe for everyday use. Current IEEE standards govern radio frequency uses from 3 kilohertz to 300 gigahertz.

Today's wireless LANs, for example, operate at 2.4 gigahertz, and typically transmit at a power level that is less than 1/1000 of a kitchen microwave oven. The exposure to radio transmissions caused by wireless networks is low compared to other items we use daily.

Security

From time to time, one hears about how a land-based computer network has been hacked. Although a hacker's job might seem easier with signals floating freely through space, wireless networking technology actually makes interception more difficult. This is because of an inherent security feature called spread-spectrum modulation. Formerly used for secure military communications, spread-spectrum modulation is used in Bluetooth, wireless LAN, and wireless WAN transmission. Spread-spectrum modulation makes the signal impossible to recover without knowing a proprietary spreading code. Wireless networks all provide data encryption, scrambling sensitive data immediately before the signal is transmitted over the air.

Encryption means the translation of data into a secret code. To read an encrypted file, you must have access to a secret key or password that enables you to decrypt it.

Many wireless LAN products, for example, include encryption features as a standard or optional component. The IEEE 802.11 standard includes a security technique known as wired equivalent privacy (WEP), which is based on the use of 64-bit keys and the popular RC4 encryption algorithm. Users without knowledge of the current key (password) will find themselves excluded from network traffic.

Cost

Businesses that implement wireless networks save money in the installation and modification of cabling infrastructure. The cost to install cabling throughout a building can be considerable and repetitive. Every time this use of space is refined or enlarged, the cabling has to be changed, as well. This can be an expensive and often chaotic process. Because most wireless networks are tied into an existing hard-wired backbone, wireless networks do not completely eliminate cables. Wireless networks do eliminate the unsightly "spaghetti" of hub-to-workstation cables.

A recent study by the Wireless LAN Association shows that on average, companies entirely recoup the cost of wireless LAN development within 12 months.

Interoperability

In theory, it is possible for wireless LAN and wireless PAN networks to interfere with each other. In reality, such interference is rare. Both networks share the same frequency bands but at dramatically different power levels and with different forms of spread-spectrum modulation. In the rather unlikely event of interference, the worst that would happen is that the error checking capability of either or both networks would kick in and signal the packets of information that have been interfered with to be retransmitted. Should this occur, the slow down would be negligible.

The two networks can be designed to work side by side at or near maximum performance.

SOME COMMON WIRELESS SOLUTIONS

Your business has its own individualized network computing needs. For the vast majority of businesses, wireless networking is the most practical solution. Depending on your wireless networking requirements, several vendors have wireless solutions that may be right for you.

Much of the rest of this book is devoted to exploring the PAN, LAN, and WAN solutions various vendors offer in depth. First, here is an overview of each.

Wireless PAN Solutions

The PDA, cell phone, notebook and desktop computers of one person or groups of people can be linked together, sharing information, via a wireless connection with the incorporation of embedded Bluetooth technology. These devices can automatically transfer updated files or information among a group of Bluetooth-enabled products just by being in the same room or data area. By mid-2003, 20 percent of mobile devices (notebook computers, PDAs, cell phones) are expected to have built-in Bluetooth technology.

Wireless LAN Solutions

The most common solution enables two PCs or notebook computers to communicate wirelessly. All you will need to do is connect your computers to a LAN system from anywhere within the wireless coverage area. Expanding or redesigning your network will be easy.

Wireless LAN technologies available today include variants of the standard called 802.11, which supports transfer rates from 2 megabits per second to 54 megabits per second, and HomeRF (home radio frequency), which supports transfer rates up to 1.6 megabits per second.

Easy-to-install wireless LAN cards from a number of vendors can also enable either two notebook or two desktop computers to communicate wirelessly without having to utilize an access point (see Figure 1-4). These cards allow you to set up small wireless workgroups for file and print sharing needs quickly. As long as the stations are within range of one another, this is the easiest and least expensive way to set up a wireless network. You will learn more about wireless LAN cards in Chapter 7.

Wireless WAN Solutions

In the most common scenario, cellular PC cards are plugged into a notebook computer/palmtop, attain a signal just like a cellular phone, and launch you right onto the Web. This will mean you have the freedom of working mobility anywhere you go if there is a cellular signal available for access.

Figure 1-4. This wireless LAN card enables computers to communicate with each other, without wires.

Hewlett Packard, for example, has teamed with Sierra Wireless and GoAmerica to provide a comprehensive solution for road warriors looking for a wireless way to tie in to their network. Hewlett Packard's WAN bundle includes the Sierra Wireless CDPD PC card and GoAmerica's service plan and compression software.

Cellular Digital Packet Data (CDPD) is a data transmission technology originally developed for use on cellular phone frequencies. CDPD uses unused cellular channels (in the 800- to 900-megahertz range) to transmit data in packets. This technology offers better error correction than using modems on an analog cellular channel. With CDPD, wireless Internet connections can be accessed at speeds up to 19.2 kilobits (19,200 bits) per second.

CHOOSING THE RIGHT WIRELESS SOLUTION

Selecting the best wireless solution for your business should largely be a matter of assessing the most mission-critical use for your wireless network.

Let us explore some of the specific uses for each technology. As you read through these uses, take note of the ones that apply to your business now or are likely to be of benefit in the near future.

PAN networks are especially helpful in enabling synchronization of notebook computers, PDAs, and cell phones. Other applications where PAN is beneficial include using your PDA to control your notebook computer presentation, sharing data/files between Bluetooth-equipped notebook computers, downloading photos from a digital camera to a notebook computer or printer, configuring a cell phone/notebook computer headset, and the use of a cell phone as a dial-up connection to your corporate network, similar to what you do today when you use your modem to dial-up via a phone line.

With Bluetooth, you would be able to perform this dial-up connection from your notebook computer to a cell phone without any intermediary cables. As Bluetooth continues to be refined, Bluetooth peripheral devices such as keyboards and mice, printers and scanners are on the way.

LANs have long been common in offices for file transfer, printer sharing, and especially shared Internet access. The appeal of a wireless LAN is obvious when you consider the difficulty and expense of laying cable and using Ethernet to wire your home or small office. You can carry your networked notebook computer to meetings and share files, printers, and Internet access when you are connected to the LAN. Typically with wireless LANs, you can be up to 150 or 200 feet away from an access point—a device that transfers data throughout the network—and still access other devices on the network. The cost of wireless LANs has recently become much more affordable.

Does your staff frequently travel for business and log on to your company server via their laptop? WAN access for notebook computers is typically used by mobile workers who need to connect to the Internet, remotely access a company network server, or connect to specialized information such as messaging, E-Mail, or paging services while traveling. If you need to communicate using your PC while you are away from your office or home without relying on a telephone or a LAN connection, look for a wireless WAN option. The range of WANs depends on the technologies used. Some work in most metropolitan areas throughout the United States but others are for specific regions only.

MOVING FORWARD

In this chapter, you been given an overview of wireless networking technologies and the business problems they solve. You have learned how wireless networking fits into business communications, the types of wireless networking technologies that are currently available, and which of these solutions might be the best for your business. You have explored issues related to security and cost, and have some useful introductory information on some of the wireless networking products and solutions several wireless networking vendors provide.

The following chapters are devoted to specific examinations of wireless networking types. In the next chapter, you learn how wireless PANs work.

CHAPTER 2

HOW WIRELESS PERSONAL AREA NETWORKS WORK

If you want to tie together the computing and communication devices in your office without wires, a wireless personal area network (PAN) is the way for you to go.

Wireless PANs either serve a small group of people or an individual user. Wireless PANs have a limited range of 33 to 35 feet, and facilitate communication among a group of personal devices like personal digital assistants (PDAs), notebooks, and cell phones in close physical proximity (see Figure 2-1). WPAN technologies are primarily intended to replace the physical cables that traditionally connect these devices, and facilitate greater data sharing and synchronization.

In this chapter, you will learn about the devices and applications that work together in PAN setups, such as in a home office or a cubicle in an office building. You will also get some useful tips about how to integrate your PAN with your local area network (LAN) or wide area network (WAN), as well as how to plan for and build your own PAN. Finally, you will get a taste of the intradevice computing and communications functions a wireless PAN can make available to you.

PANs are also sometimes referred to as private area networks. Be-

Figure 2-1. Devices communicating over a wireless PAN.

cause both references are spelled the same, PAN is the appropriate abbreviation for either.

In a wireless PAN, devices communicate with each other, as well as with standard networked and wired devices such as printers and servers. PAN communications may include the delivery of voice, data, Web applications, video clips, graphics, and more. You can also synchronize devices on a PAN so they store and work with the same collection of data. One common example of synchronization is coordinating your personal contacts on a mobile phone, notebook computer, and a PDA.

WHAT YOU CAN DO WITH A WIRELESS PAN

Personal area network applications range from file transfer to the use of cordless computer interfaces such as wireless mice, keyboards, game pads, and joysticks. PAN applications also include the use of cordless peripheral devices such as printers, access to wired LAN applications, and localized wireless LAN access. When you connect to a PAN, you can check Web sites, download E-Mail, complete file transfers, synchronize devices with corporate servers, access mobile telephones, and more. The best way to understand the benefits of a PAN is to look at some real-world applications.

The most common use of Bluetooth is to connect to the Internet via your cell phone. Every major phone manufacturer has one or more model of their phone that are Internet-ready, and for a small fee customers can have Internet access as part of their phone service. Bluetooth allows you to use your phone to extend the Internet connectivity that you have already purchased to your other Bluetooth-enabled devices. You simply connect to the Internet with your cell phone and then use Bluetooth and the dial-up networking profile to share that connection with your other Bluetooth devices. You can connect your notebook or PDA to the Internet via your cell phone in the middle of the airport or while you are at lunch.

LOOK MA—NO CABLES!

Most Bluetooth printers allow users to print without cables from a distance up to 10 meters (approximately 30 feet) away from other devices enabled for Bluetooth printing. Imagine that you are in the middle of a meeting and want to share a relevant document with other attendees. If you have your Bluetooth-enabled notebook computer with you and a printer within 30 feet or so, you can send the document to the printer without stopping to connect your notebook to that printer. The printer temporarily becomes part of your PAN. This particular solution makes it easier to move about the office and use never-before-seen devices with minimum configuration. (Tip: A Bluetooth print accessory from MPI Tech, a division of Data International A-S, enables Bluetooth wireless printing from any of several leading inkjet printers [see Figure 2-2].)

Third-party Bluetooth solutions for some PDAs enable wireless communication with other Bluetooth devices such as cell phones, printers, and PCs. For instance, you can use a Nokia mobile phone to direct a Hewlett Packard printer to print a document from the Web. Using solutions based on industry standards such as Bluetooth, the mobile phone sends the URL of a document to a Web-enabled Hewlett Packard printer. The printer retrieves the file from the Web and prints it. Nokia 9110 and 9110i Communicators currently have the capability to beam a URL using today's vCard and IR technology integrated into cell phones. Hewlett Packard printers supporting these evolving standards are now available.

During meetings and conferences, you can transfer selected documents instantly to selected participants and even exchange electronic business cards automatically without any wired connections (see Figure 2-2).

You will be able to automatically synchronize your desktop computer, mobile computer, notebook, and your mobile phone. For instance, as soon as you enter your office, the address list and calendar in your notebook automatically updates to agree with the one in your desktop, or vice versa.

You can use a Bluetooth-enabled wireless headset with a Bluetooth-enabled phone for hands-free and wire-free conversations in your car or your office. As a bonus, Bluetooth even emits much less radiation than a cell phone, so talking on the headset is a much healthier alternative to using the phone directly (see Figure 2-3).

Figure 2-2. This device enables printing over a wireless PAN.

Figure 2-3. Most Bluetooth-enabled cell phones come with a Bluetooth-enabled headset. This model is the Sony Ericsson HBH-60 Bluetooth Headset.

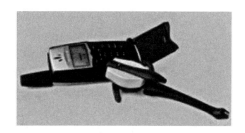

UNDERSTANDING THE BLUETOOTH–WIRELESS PAN RELATIONSHIP

Bluetooth is a standard developed by a group of electronics manufacturers that allows any type of electronic equipment from computers and cell phones to keyboards and headphones to make its own connection without wires, cables, or any direct action from a user. Bluetooth is intended to be a standard that works at two levels. First, it provides agreement at the physical level. Bluetooth is a radiofrequency standard. Second, it provides agreement at the next level, where products have to agree on when bits are sent, how many will be sent at a time, and how the parties in a conversation can be sure that the message received is the same as the message sent.

The companies belonging to the Bluetooth Special Interest Group—and there are more than one thousand of them—want to let Bluetooth's radio communications take the place of wires for connecting peripherals, telephones, and computers.

HOW WIRELESS PANs WORK WITH BLUETOOTH TECHNOLOGY

In order for you to understand how to build a wireless PAN you should understand its components. This section explores what a wireless PAN consists of. The components that constitute a WPAN are:

- One or more Bluetooth-enabled devices such as a printer or a PDA (see Figure 2-4). Under the hood of a Bluetooth-enabled device, the Bluetooth-related hardware and software components are called the Bluetooth module. The non-Bluetooth part of the device is the host. Communications between the host and the Bluetooth module are regulated by the Bluetooth module's Host Controller and by the Bluetooth Link Manager software, which authenticates the connection between two Bluetooth-enabled devices.

- The Host Controller (see Figure 2-5) manages the communication between the Bluetooth module and the host device's main circuit board. To do this, the Host Controller interfaces directly with the device's Link Controller hardware, which enables the host to synchronize with, and communicate over, a Bluetooth link.

- The Bluetooth Radio (see Figure 2-6) is at the core of the Bluetooth-enabled device. Essentially a tiny version of a broadcast transmitter, the Radio interfaces directly to the Link Controller, which then communicates with the Host Controller to the host device, such as another Bluetooth-enabled device.

Figure 2-4. Bluetooth-enabled printers do not need cables to receive files from a PC.

Figure 2-5. The Host Controller manages the communication between the Bluetooth module and the PC circuit board.

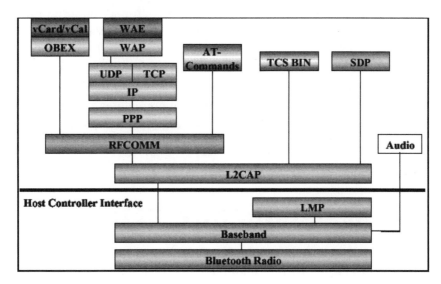

Figure 2-6. Bluetooth radios are small transmitters inside Bluetooth-enabled devices.

HOW BLUETOOTH GOT ITS NAME

Harald Bluetooth was king of Denmark around the turn of the last millennium. He united Denmark and part of Norway into a single kingdom
then introduced Christianity into Denmark. He left a large monument,
the Jelling rune stone, in memory of his parents. He was killed in 986
during a battle with his son, Svend Forkbeard. Choosing this name for
the standard indicates how important companies from the Baltic region
(nations including Denmark, Sweden, Norway, and Finland) are to the
communications industry, even if it says little about the way the technology works.

WHAT'S THE FREQUENCY, HARALD?

Bluetooth communicates on a frequency of 2.45 gigahertz, which has
been set aside by international agreement for the use of industrial, sci-
entific, and medical devices (ISM). A number of devices that you may
already use take advantage of this same radiofrequency band. Baby
monitors, garage-door openers, and the newest generation of cordless
phones all make use of frequencies in the ISM band. Making sure that
Bluetooth and these other devices do not interfere with one another has
been a crucial part of the design process.

LEARNING ABOUT ALTERNATIVES
TO BLUETOOTH

Before you decide on a Bluetooth PAN, you might want to learn about
some of the alternatives. There are in fact, a couple of ways to build a
wireless PAN without Bluetooth. It is my contention that Bluetooth is
the best choice, by far. But I think you will understand my point better
if I describe the alternatives to this easy and increasingly popular technology.

Your alternatives are infrared communications, and what is often
called cable synchronization.

Infrared sounds futuristic and a bit daunting. The term simply refers to light waves at a lower frequency than our eyes can receive, and then make sense out of. In fact, infrared is in wide use today. Think of last night, when you sat down in your living room. You picked up your remote control, and shifted channels in order to watch *The West Wing*. Your remote control system used a standard called IrDA to send an infrared pulse to your set-top control box. The invisible signal is fast, easy, and reliable (see Figure 2-7).

Similarly, a garage remote-control device sends a signal to the garage door, instructing it to open. But a funny thing happened to me the other day. A maintenance vehicle was partially blocking the line of sight between the remote control in my hand and the sensor in the garage door. I clicked, and nothing happened. Enter the bugaboo called line of sight.

Infrared uses line-of-sight technology. This technology is vulnerable to interference, or to physical blockage. That stack of papers you have in your office might stand between your PC and your printer. If so, the infrared pulse might not be able to get through.

The second drawback of infrared is that it almost always is a one-to-one technology. One-to-one simply means that you will not be able to communicate between three devices at once. You can send data between your desktop computer and your laptop computer, but not your laptop computer, desktop, and your scanner all at once.

In some ways, these two drawbacks of infrared are actually advantageous. Infrared transmitters and receivers have to be physically

Figure 2-7. TV remote-control units use IrDA to communicate with the TV set-top box.

Figure 2-8. This PDA uses a synching cradle to trade files with a PC.

lined up with each other. Because infrared communications between devices transpire only on a one-to-one basis, interference from additional devices is quite unlikely.

Cable synchronization can be a pain. Here is how it works. Picture your Pocket PC. When you want to send data from your Pocket PC PDA to your computer, you attach the PDA directly to your computer with a cable or to a synching cradle attached to your computer by means of a cable (see Figure 2-8).

Next, you press a button. This step ensures that the information on the PDA and the data on the computer match. But once again, this is a point-to-point communication that usually does not occur in real time. If you do not have access to the right file, as well as to the right computer software you will need to make the synching operation work on your PC, which could be a pain in the neck.

WHY BLUETOOTH IS BETTER

The purpose of Bluetooth is to avoid the problems that come with both infrared and cable synchronizing systems. The hardware vendors, which include Siemens, Intel, Toshiba, Motorola, and Ericsson, have developed a specification for a very small radio module to be built into computer, telephone, and entertainment equipment. From your point of view, there are three important features to Bluetooth:

1. It is wireless. When you travel, you do not have to worry about keeping track of a briefcase full of cables to attach all of your components, and you can design your road-warrior office without wondering where all the wires will go.

2. It is inexpensive. Prices are coming down.

3. You do not have to think about it. Look at it this way: you have plenty more to think about when you are on the road. Bluetooth does not require you to do anything special to make it work. The devices find one another and strike up a conversation without any user input at all.

NO STATIC AT ALL

One of the ways Bluetooth devices avoid interfering with other systems is by sending out very weak signals of 1 milliwatt. By comparison, the most powerful cell phones can transmit a signal of 3 watts. The low power limits the range of a Bluetooth device to approximately 30 to 33 feet, reducing the chances of interference between your computer system and your portable telephone or television in the next room. Even with the low power, the walls in your house—unlike physical objects that can thwart infrared transmissions—will not stop a Bluetooth signal. This makes the Bluetooth standard useful for controlling several devices in different rooms.

There is actually a very interesting explanation for the lack of static Bluetooth devices produce.

With many different Bluetooth devices in a room, you might think they would interfere with one another. The trick is these devices will not be on the same frequency at the same time. That is because Bluetooth uses a technique called spread-spectrum frequency hopping. In this technique, a device will use as many as 79 individual randomly

Figure 2-9. Bluetooth-enabled transmitters
change frequency 1,600 times per second.

chosen frequencies within a designated range. These frequencies will
switch from one to another on a regular basis, and at lightning speed.

In the case of Bluetooth, the transmitters (see Figure 2-9) change
frequencies 1,600 times every second, meaning that more devices can
make full use of a limited slice of the radio spectrum. Because every
Bluetooth transmitter uses spread-spectrum transmitting automatically, the odds are several thousand-to-one that any two Bluetooth-enabled transmitters will be on the same frequency at the same time. This
same technique minimizes the risk that portable phones or baby monitors will disrupt Bluetooth devices, because any interference on a particular frequency will last only a tiny fraction of a second.

IT HAPPENS AUTOMATICALLY

When Bluetooth-capable devices come within range of one another, an
electronic "conversation" takes place to determine whether they have
data to share or whether one device needs to control the other. This
happens automatically. You do not have to press a button or issue a keyboard command to the device.

Once the conversation has taken place, the devices form a network.
Bluetooth systems create a PAN or piconet (see Figure 2-10) that
might fill a room or might encompass no more distance than that be-

tween the cell phone on a belt-clip and the headset on your head. Once a piconet is established, the members randomly hop frequencies in unison so they stay in touch with one another and avoid other piconets that may be operating in the same room.

Here is a bit more information about how the signal hopping makes interference unlikely. Different devices send radio signals asking for a response from any units with an address in a particular range. If they receive signals from other devices not in the network, such as a remote phone in the next room, they ignore that pulse. Once the networks are established, the systems begin talking among themselves. Each piconet hops randomly through the available frequencies, so all of the piconets are completely separated from one another.

If by some remote chance, your Bluetooth-enabled wireless PAN picks up a "foreign" transmission, it will only do so for a fraction of a second, then the signal will change. Additionally, the software inside most Bluetooth devices is designed to detect and weed out the unwelcome signal.

Figure 2-10. Bluetooth devices form a piconet to communicate over a wireless PAN.

WHAT HAPPENS NEXT

When new Bluetooth-capable devices come within range of one another, an electronic conversation takes place to determine whether they have data to share or whether one needs to control the other. You do not have to press a button or give a command: the electronic conversation happens automatically. Once the conversation has occurred, the devices—whether they are part of a computer system or a stereo—form a network.

A connection between two Bluetooth-enabled devices is called a link. For Bluetooth-enabled devices to function within a link, these devices need to be equipped with Link Manager software (see Figure 2-11) configured to work with Link Controller hardware. Link Manager software manages the link setup, configuration, and security related

Figure 2-11. Link Manager software enables Bluetooth devices to communicate over a wireless PAN.

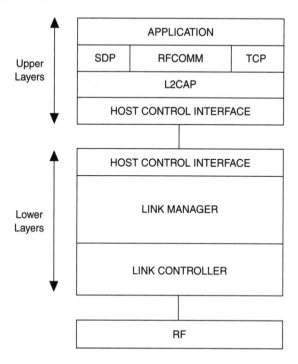

authentication necessary for two Bluetooth devices to link. Essentially, the authentication procedure validates that each machine is able to communicate with the other. Link Manager software does this by discovering other devices within reception range that are running on the same Link Manager software (such as a PDA and a printer).

This exchange is carried out via the Link Manager Protocol, a type of communications management language used by Bluetooth devices. The Link Manager Protocol regulates such functions as encryption of secure data, the size of packets within a message, and the power settings necessary for the radios within the Bluetooth devices to communicate efficiently with each other.

When the software detects a compatible Bluetooth-enabled device, the program sends a kind of "let's talk" message to the Link Controller hardware in the target device. In turn, when the Link Controller hardware recognizes that one of its authorized brethren is attempting to communicate with it, the hardware instructs the Link Controller software to start exchanging data with the other device. This establishes the link between the two devices.

UNDERSTANDING DUPLEX

Most of the time, a network or communications method either works in one direction at a time (half-duplex communication) or in both directions simultaneously (full-duplex communication). A speakerphone that lets you either listen or talk, but not both, is an example of half-duplex communication, while a regular telephone handset is a full-duplex device.

Because Bluetooth is designed to work in a number of different circumstances, it can be either half-duplex or full-duplex. A cordless telephone is an example of a use that will call for a full-duplex (two-way) link. Bluetooth can send data at more than 64,000 bits per second in a full-duplex link—a rate high enough to support several human voice conversations. If a particular use calls for a half-duplex link, for example, connecting to a computer printer, Bluetooth can transmit up to 721 kilobits per second in one direction, with 57.6 kilobits per second in the other. If the use calls for the same speed in both directions, a link with a 432.6-kilobit capacity in each direction can be made.

UNDERSTANDING BLUETOOTH PROFILES

Chances are the Bluetooth-enabled devices that make up the PAN you are participating in at any given moment from conference room to cubicle will not all be from the same manufacturer. Even though all of these devices use the same standard to communicate they need just a little more help to get real work such as printing, file transfer, and dial-up networking done.

This help comes in the form of standardized Bluetooth profiles. A profile holds all of the information two or more devices need to work together to perform a real-world task such as printing a document stored on a Bluetooth-enabled notebook on a Bluetooth-enabled printer. In this particular example the printing profile helps the notebook and the printer exchange the relevant information that each needs to make the printing actually happen.

Bluetooth-enabled devices come with a variety of these profiles built into them. After all, what good is a Bluetooth-enabled printer without the printing profile? As new profiles are released, the Bluetooth devices can be upgraded to support these new profiles.

Speaking of upgrades, the Microsoft XP operating system includes support for Bluetooth and has a healthy collection of standard profiles including printing and file transfer.

The printing profile has already been mentioned as an example of the kind of profiles you can expect your Bluetooth devices to support. Another important profile is the one that facilitates dial-up networking via a cell phone or PDA. You can use the wireless modem in your cell phone or PDA to connect to the Internet and then share that connectivity with other devices in your PAN.

The goal behind profiles is to make it as easy as possible to take advantage of your Bluetooth-enabled wireless PAN. Profiles make it possible to turn on your Bluetooth-enabled computer, see a list of devices currently sharing your wireless PAN, and then click on each individual device to see what kind of services (printing, networking, file transfer, etc.) are available for that device. You probably will not be surprised to know that a service discovery profile makes this particular functionality tick.

Some other profiles already available or in development include:

- The LAN access profile

- The fax profile

- The synchronization profile

In the final analysis, profiles are what make Bluetooth easy to use because they manage all of the behind-the-scenes activities that are required for wireless devices to work together.

A good resource for learning more about all aspects of Bluetooth is the site run by the minds behind the Bluetooth standard. Visit *bluetooth.com* for more information on this important technology.

ADDING BLUETOOTH TO COMPUTERS THAT ARE NOT ALREADY BLUETOOTH-ENABLED

If you have a notebook computer without built-in Bluetooth capability, you can enable that function with just a few steps and a PCMCIA Bluetooth card. The card works with Windows 98 Special Edition, Windows Millennium, Windows 2000, and Windows XP. It is compatible with many notebook and desktop PCs.

INTEGRATING WIRELESS PANs WITH WIRELESS LANs

While the terminology sounds complicated and the alphabet soup of abbreviated terms is definitely present, Bluetooth-enabled devices can easily be configured to interface with your LAN. The key to connecting a Bluetooth-enabled device to a LAN—wireless or wired—is the LAN access point, a data terminal connected to the LAN.

In one common integration scenario, you bring your Bluetooth-enabled laptop computer to work with you. As you turn on the device, it automatically detects the presence of an office network. It then connects to the LAN via the closest or most available LAN access point. This happens automatically. The old wired solution, which involved a hit-and-miss procedure with a network jack and an Ethernet card and cable, was anything but automatic.

The automatic LAN access point connection occurs because the access point's address can be pre-entered into Bluetooth-enabled devices. The process is governed by a Master switch inside the specific Bluetooth device (see Figure 2-12), which hands off the data being exchanged to the LAN access point.

Figure 2-12. A Master Switch controls the connection between a wireless PAN

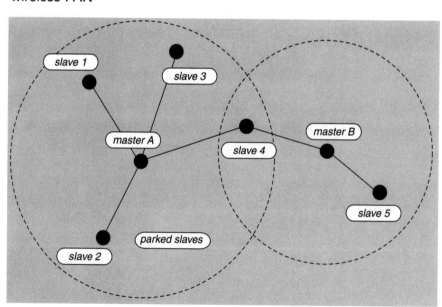

In order to connect to the LAN access point, your Bluetooth-enabled device must find it first. Your device makes the connection by sending a signal to the LAN access point. Some LANs have multiple LAN access points. If this is the case, then the Master will search for the LAN access point that is the least occupied with unrelated data traffic or other duties. This pickiness serves a noble purpose: the freer the LAN access point, the better performance in terms of speedy data exchange.

Finally, in order for the LAN access point to accept communications from your Bluetooth-enabled device, the access point needs to be equipped with a Slave switch. LANs equipped with Slave switches will be able to automatically instruct the LAN access point to regulate the wireless communications.

A REVIEW OF BLUETOOTH SPECS

Here are some specification details from the Bluetooth Web site. These will be useful as you plan and build your Bluetooth-enabled, wireless PAN.

The devices in a piconet share a common communication data channel. The channel has a total capacity of 1 megabit per second. Headers and handshaking information consume approximately 20 percent of this capacity.

In the United States and Europe, the frequency range is 2,400 to 2,483.5 megahertz, with seventy-nine 1-megahertz radiofrequency channels. In practice, the range is 2,402 megahertz to 2,480 megahertz. In Japan, the frequency range is 2,472 to 2,497 megahertz with twenty-three 1-megahertz radiofrequency channels.

A data channel hops randomly 1,600 times per second between the 79 nine (or 23) RF channels.

Each channel is divided into time slots that are 625 microseconds long.

A piconet has a Master and up to seven Slaves. The Master transmits in even time slots, Slaves in odd time slots.

Packets can be up to five time slots wide.

Data in a packet can be up to 2,745 bits in length.

There are currently two types of data transfer between devices: Synchronous Connection Oriented (SCO) and Asynchronous Connectionless (ACL).

In a piconet, there can be up to three SCO links of 64,000 bits per second each. To avoid timing and collision problems, the SCO links use reserved slots set up by the Master.

Masters can support up to three SCO links with one, two, or three Slaves.

Slots not reserved for SCO links can be used for ACL links.

One Master and Slave can have a single ACL link.

ACL is either point-to-point (Master to one Slave) or broadcast to all the Slaves.

ACL Slaves can only transmit when requested by the Master.

WHAT YOU HAVE LEARNED

Wireless Personal Area Networks, or WPANs, are not the same thing as Wireless Local Area Networks, or WLANs.

WLANs tie one or more devices equipped with wireless capability to a wired network, or even to the Internet. WPANs, on the other hand, have a limited range at maximum, 33 to 35 feet, and facilitate communication among a group of personal devices like PDAs, notebooks, and cell phones in close physical proximity. They usually accomplish this by means of devices equipped to send and receive signals running the Bluetooth wireless specification.

Wireless PAN technologies are primarily intended to replace the physical cables that traditionally connect these devices, and facilitate greater data sharing and synchronization.

In this chapter, you have learned about the devices and applications that work together in PAN setups—such as in a home office or a cubicle in an office building. Hopefully, you also picked up some useful tips about how to integrate your PAN with your Local Area Network (LAN) or Wide Area Network (WAN), as well as how to plan for and build your own PAN.

Finally, reading this chapter gave you a taste of the intra-device computing and communications functions a wireless PAN can make available to you.

CHAPTER 3

HOW WIRELESS LOCAL AREA NETWORKS WORK

This chapter explains the devices and applications that work together in a wireless local area network (LAN). It begins with a discussion of the components that make up a wireless LAN and the functions they enable. You will learn how seamlessly you can integrate your wireless LAN with your wired LAN. You will also learn how to plan for and construct a wireless LAN and how to manage it once it is built.

Finally, you will read about some wireless LAN solutions that will equip your desktops, notebooks, personal digital assistants (PDAs), and printers with wireless LAN capability—even if that capability was not built into the unit at the time of manufacture.

BENEFITS OF A WIRELESS LAN

When your notebook is set up for wireless access, you can take your notebook computer, walk around your office, and access whatever is on your wired LAN (because your wired LAN is hooked up to your wireless LAN) as long as you are within proximity of the access point. You might wish to access your E-Mail, an Excel spreadsheet, a PowerPoint presentation, or material you are exporting from your company database.

In another common application, you may wish to transfer files from your PDA to your wired LAN for printout or distribution across your company Intranet. You can do this by connecting your wired LAN-equipped device to your wireless LAN, and then to the access point where the wireless LAN integrates with your wired LAN.

Figure 3-1. A wireless LAN enables you to get easy network access in conference rooms or hard-to-wire areas.

In the case of a desktop PC, a wireless LAN enables you to get network access into conference rooms or hard-to-wire areas without having to crawl under a desk or maneuvering into tight corners (see Figure 3-1).

HOW WIRELESS LANs COMMUNICATE

Wireless LANs operate by using electromagnetic radio or infrared airwaves to send information from one point to another without using a physical connection. Because these airwaves carry the signal, these airwaves are collectively known as radio carriers. The carrier adjusts to transmit at specific frequencies based on the data it is trying to transmit and the device to which it is trying to transmit.

For devices on a wireless LAN to communicate, they all have to speak the same language. Communication standards define the language that the devices speak. If two devices do not support the same standards, they cannot participate in the same wireless LAN. Of the available standards, the Institute of Electrical and Electronic Engineers (IEEE) 802.11b standard is the market standard. Most current wireless LAN solutions are built around IEEE 802.11b rather than HomeRF.

IEEE 802.11b capabilities include data transfer speeds of 11 megabits per second, which is equivalent to a wired LAN. Because IEEE 802.11b devices are able to break bits of transmitted data into small chunks, called frames, the data being exchanged on the wireless LAN can be managed more efficiently and is less subject to interference. The lack of interference actually improves transmission speed.

End users access the wireless LAN through IEEE 802.11b-enabled wireless LAN adapters. Adapters use an antenna (see Figure 3-2) to retrieve data from airwaves and convey it to the network operating system. These adapters come in the form of PC cards in notebook computers, ISA or PCI adapters for desktop computers, and adapters within smaller devices.

Wireless LANs with devices configured for the IEEE 802.11b standard can easily accommodate forty to sixty users, and even more in some cases.

Figure 3-2. The antenna in this wireless LAN adapter ensures access to the wireless network. Courtesy, D-Link Systems, Inc.

HOW WIRELESS LANs ARE CONFIGURED

In one of the most common LAN configurations, the access point hooks up to the wired LAN via an Ethernet cable. A single access point can support a group of users within a few hundred feet of the point. The antenna attached to the access point needs to be placed in a position where the wireless LAN can be received without blockage or static (see Figure 3-3).

Figure 3-3. This access point antenna is in the best position to send and receive signals over the wireless LAN.

Wireless LANs can either be used to create a completely wireless network, or as an extension to your wired LAN. In the real world, you probably will not switch from a wired LAN to a wireless LAN overnight, but will instead integrate wireless into your network as it makes sense and meets your needs.

WHAT IS INSIDE A WIRELESS LAN

The technology behind a wireless LAN integration into a wired LAN includes:

- A notebook computer or other device that is wireless enabled (see Figure 3-4).

- Access points for both the wired and wireless LAN (see Figure 3-5).

- A server for the wired LAN (see Figure 3-6).

Wireless-enabled devices come in two types: those that are built with wireless networking functionality embedded in them and those that have it added to them later. A variety of notebook PCs, PDAs, printers, and other devices from several manufacturers come with wireless functionality built right in. If you have a device that is not wireless-ready, you can make it ready pretty easily.

Figure 3-4. This Hewlett Packard Deskjet 450cbi printer is wireless-network enabled.

Figure 3-5. This AmbiCom Access Point is one of several popular AP's in use on wireless networks.

Figure 3-6. The server in this diagram works with a wired LAN.

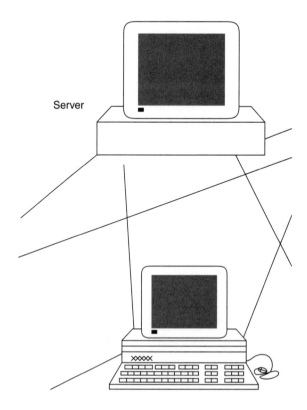

Server

NIC KNACK

Wireless network interface cards (NICs) fit into the PC card slots of notebook computers, and PCI cards or universal serial bus (USB) devices are available for stationary computers (see Figure 3-7). Sometimes referred to as Ethernet cards, wireless LAN PC cards generally come equipped with small antennas. There are even add-ons for PDAs and printers to make them wireless-ready.

The center of the wireless-wired LAN connectivity is the wireless access point (see Figure 3-8). These points aggregate wireless radio signals and then connect the two LANs. The access point is generally book-sized. It contains a radio transceiver, communications and encryption software, and an Ethernet port for a cable connection to a hub or switch on the wired LAN.

The radio transceiver built into the access point negotiates a connection between the end user and the wired LAN, hooking the user up to the LAN in the same way a cable would (see Figure 3-9). The greater the distance from the computer to the access point, the poorer the signal and the slower the connection. Because of this limitation, large offices often deploy several access points with overlapping ranges. In an open-space environment free of obstruction, access

Figure 3-7. PCI cards enable desktop computers to function in a wireless LAN.

Figure 3-8. The wireless Access Point is at the hub of this wireless LAN.

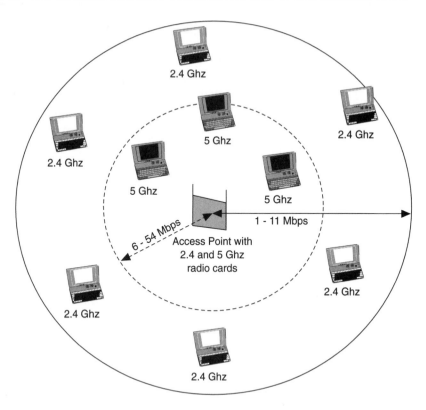

Figure 3-9. A radio transceiver is built into this Hewlett Packard hn 230w wireless network Access Point.

points can be as much as three hundred feet apart. Where walls and ceilings jut out, fifty feet is a useful maximum range.

Because the performance of an access point is subject to these structural variances, most wireless LAN products come with site survey and configuration utilities to help you decide how many access points you need and where to put them.

A LA MODES

Unlike wired networks, wireless networks have two different modes in which they can be set up. These modes are Infrastructure Mode, and Ad-Hoc mode.

If the computers on the wireless network need to be accessible by a wired network or need to share a peripheral such as a printer with the wired network computers, the wireless network should be set up in the Infrastructure mode. Infrastructure mode is built around an access point. The access point serves as the main point of communications for the wireless LAN, and transmits data to PCs equipped with wireless network adapters.

You should choose Ad-Hoc mode only if you are not attaching any wired devices to your wireless network.

STEPS YOU WILL NEED TO TAKE

There is no single way to build a wireless LAN. The information in the following section should help you become familiar with the steps you will need to pursue to plan for, and then build, your wireless LAN.

These steps include:

- Determining the number of users who will need to have access to your wireless network.

- Identifying the equipment you will need.

- Planning for the connection between your wireless LAN and your wired LAN.

- Configuring your wireless devices to work with your network.

- Testing the installation before it goes live.

- Establishing a procedure to manage your wireless LAN.

How Many Users Will You Serve?

This step is partially dependent on the in-office communication needs of your business, as well as the practical limits of various access point hardware. As a rule of thumb, fifty users often is a workable limit.

The Equipment You Will Need

Before you can build your wireless LAN, you need to determine what equipment you want to buy. Your shopping list should include wireless-enabled devices such as wireless notebook computers, access points, wireless LAN adapters, and wireless cards. The quantity of equipment you buy will depend on the number of users that you will have. For example, the Hewlett Packard Enterprise Access Point can support up to fifty users (see Figure 3-10).

Installing Your Access Point

You will next need to determine where to install the access point. Ideally, you would probably want a professional to do this, because they

Figure 3-10. The Hewlett Packard Enterprise Access Point can support up to fifty users.

could design a network that would give you maximum range within your building. However, it is very easy to do it yourself as well.

You probably want to install your access point in a central location since there is a "wireless sphere" around it. This maximizes the wireless range. You also want to make sure that the access point is installed in as open an environment as possible, so that there are not many obstacles between the access point and usage points.

Installing the access point to the wired LAN requires you to plug in an Ethernet cable to it and configure it (see Figure 3-11). The configuration process includes using software that ships with the access point to assign a network name and an encryption key.

Testing Your Installation

Once you acquire and configure all of your equipment, you should test your new wireless setup. A good test would not be unlike a rehearsal for a play. With several users and devices, work up a realistic scenario for an exchange of wireless LAN data. Using link test software provided by such vendors as Agilent Technologies, you should test for such criteria as the percent of data sent correctly, the time it takes to re-

Figure 3-11. Using an Ethernet cable to hook up an Intermec 2100 Universal Access Point to a wired LAN.

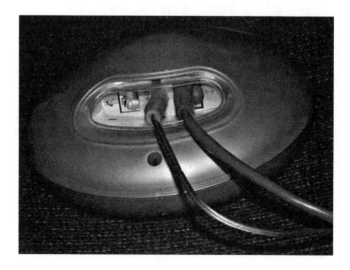

ceive a response from the destination device, and the strength of the transmitted signal.

The distance that radiofrequency and infrared signals can travel is a function of product design including transmitted power, receiver design, and antenna design and obstacles in the propagation path, especially in indoor environments. Interactions with typical building objects, including walls, metal, and even people, can affect how the signal propagates and thus what range and coverage a particular system achieves. Solid objects block an infrared signal, which imposes additional limitations and makes the technology difficult to use in the real world.

Devices can communicate only if they have line-of-sight, that is, the path that the infrared wave travels is unobstructed. Most wireless LAN systems use radiofrequency because radio waves can penetrate most indoor walls and obstacles. The range (or radius of coverage) for typical wireless LAN access point varies from less than one hundred feet to a little more than three hundred feet. That is ten times farther than Bluetooth, but we are talking different technologies here. However, as the range increases, the speed of the connection degrades. For optimal performance, coverage can be extended, and true freedom of mobility via roaming is provided through microcells.

Managing Your Wireless LAN

Once you have a wireless LAN in place, you should ensure its efficient operation that meets your network's standards. Maintaining these standards is a matter of efficiently managing technologies, processes, and people.

Training is an essential component of wireless LAN management. Your system administrators, maintenance staff, and end users within your LAN should each be taught how to use the network, its accompanying hardware and software, and how to diagnose problems when they arise.

If you are a mid- to large-size user, you should consider establishing a help desk for end users who may be frustrated with wireless LAN-related problems. If you are not able to establish a help desk specifically for networking issues, then designate one or more people within your company for ad hoc help desk duty. Make that phone number or extension known to your switchboard operator and post it on your company Intranet.

Systems administrators should receive enhanced training. The prepared systems administrator will, at minimum, need to understand how the network is configured—including the specific setting each device on the wireless LAN needs in order to communicate with the other, and with the access point or points on the wired LAN.

System administrators should also be assigned periodic help desk duty. Such responsibilities will give them a real-world sense of the questions the wireless LAN end users are liable to ask. In doing so, they will be able to more directly identify and fix any systemic problems or glitches.

MONITORING YOUR WIRELESS LAN'S PERFORMANCE

As your wireless LAN runs, you will also need to monitor the network. Once again, the solution is part technology and part procedural. On the technology front, you should be aware that wireless network access points and radio cards inside networked devices maintain a management information base. This base stores statistics such as transmission failures and errors. You can monitor this management information base with a network monitoring station, such as one of the several Observer brands of network analysis and management tools made by Network Instruments, LLC.

Even with these tools in place, do not overlook preventive maintenance at varied intervals. Whether your maintenance staff is in-house or a third party, you need to train them on where your network access points are. Keep plenty of documentation around, as well as spare LAN-enabled end devices should one fail. Problems do not happen often, but when a wireless LAN fails, it can be because of something wrong within one of the devices in the network. If you are thinking of the spare tire in your trunk as a metaphor, you are right.

EXTENDING YOUR WIRELESS LAN

Wireless LAN communication is limited by how far signals carry for given power output. If your enterprise is located in several attached buildings, it may be time to consider expanding your wireless LAN by constructing several of them, and then connecting them with each other. In most cases, this will mean constructing a wireless wide area network (WAN). Wireless WANs are discussed in Chapter 4.

WHAT YOU HAVE LEARNED

By reading this chapter, you have become familiar with the devices and applications that work together in a wireless Local Area Network (LAN).

The chapter started out with a discussion of the components that make up a wireless LAN and the functions they enable. These components include one or more wireless-enabled devices, such as a notebook computer with a wireless LAN card; an Access Point to tie your wireless network to your wired network, and a server for your wired LAN. By careful planning, you can integrate your wireless LAN with your wired LAN.

In this chapter, you also read about some wireless LAN solutions that will equip your desktops, notebooks, PDAs, and printers with wireless LAN capability. Even though many new devices on the market come with this built-in capability, other models do not. That is why it will be helpful for you to master the process of upgrading your potential wireless networking components for the task.

CHAPTER 4

HOW WIRELESS WIDE AREA NETWORKS WORK

Wireless wide area networks (WANs), which can bridge branch offices of a company, cover a much more extensive area than wireless local area networks (LANs). Unlike wireless LANs, which are generally used to enable the mobility within a building or limited space, wireless WANs can encompass different areas within large office complexes, or even within metropolitan areas. Unlike wireless LANs, the coverage area for wireless WANs is normally measured in miles rather than feet.

Wireless WANs use coverage cells (microcells) created by access points, similar to the cellular telephone system, to extend the range of wireless connectivity. At any point in time, a mobile PC equipped with a wireless network adapter is associated with a single access point and its microcell or an area of coverage. Individual microcells overlap to enable continuous communication within a wired network. They handle low-power signals and hand off users as they roam through a given geographic area.

Multiple microcells are created by using multiple access points to create several coverage areas—sometimes overlapping—that allow for coverage of the enterprise. Creating overlap provides an added benefit: the wireless network card will automatically select the access point that provides the best service, speed, and reliability. This ensures the coverage area has no gaps in coverage and a level of redundancy.

A typical mixed wired/wireless LAN configuration is similar to the cellular phone system you use. The Ethernet-wired LAN functions as a backbone line that interconnects all access points. In functionality, it resembles those ugly cell phone towers that dot your city and the surrounding landscape.

Roaming across different wireless LAN cells is supported as part of the Institute of Electrical and Electronics Engineers IEEE 802.11 standard, much the same way as driving through multiple cellular coverage cells allows for seamless roaming.

In most wireless LAN applications with multiple access points, your employees or other users should be able to maintain a continuous connection while roaming from one physical area to another. Nearly all wireless LAN manufacturers support this kind of roaming through a process by which the mobile nodes automatically register with the new access point.

PLANNING WIRELESS WANs FOR YOUR MOBILE USERS

If your roaming wireless users sit down, turn on their portable computers, establish a wireless networking session, conduct their business, log off, and then turn off their machines, mobility may not be an issue. If your users need continuous access to your network, consider a wireless WAN because wireless WANs allow users to maintain access to work-related applications and information while away from their office.

WHY YOU MAY NEED A WIRELESS WAN

Many enterprises are frustrated by the bandwidth bottleneck because they have branch offices, factories, or warehouses located outside the urban core, where high-speed access is relatively cheap and plentiful.

For example, a company's downtown headquarters may well be the only enterprise location in the metropolitan area with high-speed data connections.

Operating LAN facilities at multiple remote locations presents a significant internetworking challenge. Employees at a suburban warehouse or a factory across town are isolated not only from high-speed Internet access, but also from the large databases on corporate LAN servers.

Wireless WAN connectivity means hospitals can track patients and their charts remotely. Sales staff has access to the latest product information for customer presentations. Managers can get the latest data to make decisions when they are away from their offices. Public safety officials can have access to data while they are in the field.

It is access to data communications connections wherever and whenever they are needed that is driving the market. Dataquest Inc., the San Jose-based research firm, projects that the wireless data market will reach 36 million in 2003. Cahners In-Stat's projections are slightly lower. Both research firms agree, however, that in the near term, it is corporate users who will drive this growth. This business demand will eventually lower future wireless access costs and open the doors to the consumer market.

Wireless Internet provider (IP) links ideally extend the individual enterprise LANs into a metropolitan enterprise WAN with minimum additional equipment and cost. Free E-Mail transport and low-cost voice-over-IP telephone access or PBX extensions can be furnished to all locations on the enterprise WAN. This application can be even more compelling in international markets, where satellite offices typically wait years for even basic telephone service. Most enterprises will turn to a local carrier to provide the actual wireless link. This, in turn, creates new business opportunities.

HOW WIRELESS WANs WORK

Wireless WAN connectivity requires wireless modems and a wireless network infrastructure, provided as a for-fee service by a wireless service carrier such as GoAmerica. Portable devices receive communications as the connected wireless modems and wireless networks interact via radio waves. The modem directly interfaces with radio towers, which carry the signal to a mobile switching center, where the signal is passed on to the appropriate public or private network link (i.e., telephone, other high-speed line, or even the Internet) (see Figure 4-1). From here, the signal can be transferred to an organization's existing network. Users can retrieve E-Mail, Web pages, data, and more.

In wireless WANs, communication occurs predominantly through the use of radio signals over analog, digital cellular, or PCS networks, although signal transmission through microwaves and other electromagnetic waves is also possible. Although traditional analog networks, having been designed for voice rather than data transfer, have some inherent problems, some 2G (second generation) and new third-genera-

Figure 4-1. This Nokia 2G/3G Mobile Switching Center handles wireless WAN communications.

tion (3G) digital cellular networks are fully integrated for data and voice transmission. With the advent of 3G networks, transfer speeds have increased greatly.

WIRELESS WANs AND THE INTERNET

Wireless WANs also give users access to the Internet. For small devices such as personal digital assistants (PDAs) and mobile phones, a universal specification known as wireless application protocol (WAP) exists to facilitate the delivery and presentation of Web content. The request for Web content is sent through the wireless network to a WAP gateway, where it is processed and the required information is retrieved and returned, much like what happens when a Web browser requests and receives a Web page. Most wireless networks and mobile device operating systems support WAP.

ACCESSING YOUR WIRELESS WAN WITH A WIRELESS DEVICE

Accessing a wireless WAN with your favorite wireless devices is very simple. Just install the software that ships with the wireless connectivity accessory—usually a plug-and-play card—onto your device, whether PDA or notebook computer, and you are ready to go. You also need to sign up for service with a network service provider. Often, that specific provider will have a pricing special offered in league with your notebook computer manufacturer.

Chances are, your notebook computer or PDA did not come with wireless WAN access built in. Only selected such devices available in the last year or so have included this functionality. Even so, you do not necessarily have to buy the hardware separately. Often you can call the service provider, sign up for service, and get the PCMCIA (Personal Computer Memory Card International Association) card or other hardware you need at a discounted price.

In just one example, Hewlett Packard currently uses GoAmerica for wireless WAN service for notebook computers and some handheld PCs. You activate wireless WAN service in the same way you access cell phone service. You give the provider information about your specific hardware and they activate the service for you. Even rate plans resemble cell phone rate plans.

GoAmerica Go.Web technology allows their customers to browse the Internet and access customizable Internet content, including business and financial news, sports, weather, stock, and travel updates virtually anywhere, anytime. The service also enables users to optimize time spent on the Internet by controlling E-Mail attachments and limiting graphics while browsing.

BLUEPRINT FOR A WIRELESS WAN

You would be surprised at how quickly you can set up and start using a wireless WAN. First, get your devices ready to access the WAN. Install the wireless enabling product—usually a PCMCIA card—on your notebook (see Figure 4-2). Next call the service provider recommended by the manufacturer of your notebook computer or PDA and sign up for a service plan with them. It is important to remember, however, that these first two steps only give you access to the general Internet and not to your organization's network.

However, most corporations will have some kind of virtual private network (VPN) solution that you use in conjunction with remote access. Once you are logged on to the Internet, you can get access to

Figure 4-2. To ensure your notebook computer is wireless enabled, insert a PCMCIA card such as this 3Com model.

your corporate network via VPN, and you will have access to your organization's LAN-wired, wireless, or both.

BUILDING-TO-BUILDING WIRELESS WANs

Without a wired alternative, organizations frequently resort to WAN technologies to link together separate LANs. Contracting with a local telephone provider for a leased line presents a variety of drawbacks. Installation is typically expensive and rarely immediate. Monthly fees are often quite high for bandwidth that by LAN standards is very low. A wireless bridge can be purchased and then installed in less time and at a fraction of the cost. Once the initial hardware investment is made, there are no recurring charges, and today's wireless bridges provide the bandwidth one would expect from a technology rooted in data, rather than voice, communications.

In the same way that a commercial radio signal can be picked up in all sorts of weather miles from its transmitter, wireless LAN technology applies the power of radio waves to truly redefine the "local" in LAN. With a wireless bridge, networks located in buildings several miles from each other can be integrated into a single LAN. When bridging between buildings with traditional copper or fiber optic cable, freeways, lakes, and even local governments can be impassible obstacles. A wireless bridge is a small device that acts as a wireless transmitter and receiver, and it transmits data through the air and requires no license or other permit.

Wireless LAN technology is also used for bridging conventional wired networks together, which can be particularly useful if two sites have a line of sight with each other and the only wired bridging option involves monthly service charges to a telecommunications company or other network provider. Many wireless LAN vendors offer bridging products based on the same spread spectrum technology as their wireless LANs. Using them is quite straightforward. First, you need to determine whether to use directional antennas, effective to about one hundred meters, or directed antennas for a greater range. These antennas can easily cover distances of over a mile and with amplification (which is now allowed under recently relaxed Federal Communications Commission rules) can reach as far as 25 miles.

Specified throughputs range from 1 megabits per second to 10 megabits per second, depending on the product offering and price. The actual throughput will be less. In testing, 10 megabits per second bridges show throughputs of just over 5 megabits per second. After taking into account the range and throughput, consider any other bridging requirements you may have, such as support for routing and specific protocols. The cost of wireless connectivity at 5 megabits per second is considerably less than the cost of wired connectivity at 5 megabits per second.

To achieve building-to-building wireless connectivity, a wireless networking bridge provided with directional antennas requires a line-of sight connection. This configuration can facilitate wireless WAN networking at distances of up to one mile. Once the additional antennas are installed, all that is required is to connect the network to the wireless access points and configure the settings. This enables wireless LAN connectivity in a campus environment with multiple buildings.

UNDERSTANDING WIRELESS WAN LIMITATIONS

The demand for connecting mobile devices to content-rich networks is rising quickly; and it would seem that wireless WAN technology is the perfect answer. But today's wireless WANs have limitations in several areas, including security, performance, application persistence, roaming, and compatibility with off-the-shelf applications. Finally, because the wireless WAN is "spread out," there are significant management and control issues that must be addressed.

The best way to illustrate the technical solutions for these dilemmas is by selecting (but not necessarily endorsing) a typical wireless WAN solution provider suite. There are numerous providers offering these authentication solutions. In this case, we have chosen NetMotion Mobility, from NetMotion Wireless, Inc. (see Figure 4-3).

Figure 4-3. Implementing the global settings in the NetMotion Mobility wireless networking software.

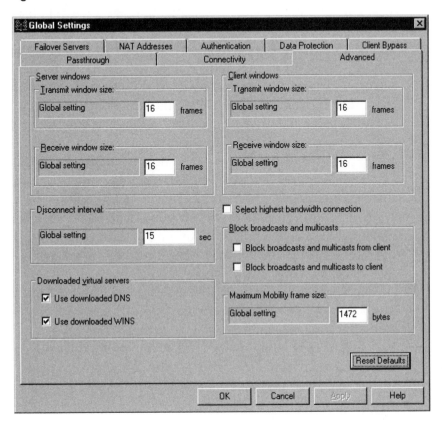

WIRELESS WAN SECURITY CONCERNS AND SOLUTIONS

In modern network topologies, physical boundaries between public and private networks are blurring. When a company decides to add wireless connectivity to this mix, they must protect their information security. Wireless systems in general broadcast data over radio waves into the ether. The security implications are obvious: what companies broadcast goes everywhere. One of the first concerns that the Information Technology (IT) department has is whether the information crossing the wireless network boundary is secure, because it is susceptible to eavesdropping. Second, they must feel confident that a user has the necessary network permissions to access information, because they cannot rely on the mobile device's physical location to tell them. Devices connected wirelessly can easily breech two of the most fundamental network security policies: authentication and confidentiality.

With solution providers such as NetMotion Mobility, each user is authenticated by the corporate network. All transmissions are then optionally encrypted using industry standards—AES (the Advanced Encryption Standard for the United States, a 128-bit algorithm also known as Rijndael); Twofish (128-bit encryption); triple-DES (112-bit encryption); or DES (56-bit encryption)—and then compressed again using standard deflate/inflate algorithms, similar to a VPN. But you do not have to worry about all that stuff. Much of this crunching happens automatically, under the hood.

NetMotion Mobility further integrates the standard user and group attributes with the Microsoft Windows 2000 and Windows NT security system. Using these standards enables NetMotion to provide a high degree of security and a greater level of centralized control than other wireless systems, and it also means that the workload and learning curve of the information manager is reduced.

WIRELESS WAN PERFORMANCE CONCERNS AND SOLUTIONS

Today's standard network topologies and protocol implementations were designed for communications between stationary systems. In general, when a mobile device communicates with a stationary device, the stationary system uses the same algorithms to communicate with its mobile peer. It is not aware that the device is mobile, and it is this lack of awareness that is at the heart of most performance problems.

All sorts of circumstances never encountered in wired infrastructures affect wireless connections: environmental factors such as user movement, harmonics, terrain, and weather can easily affect through-put and performance. Application performance can further degrade when generic transport implementations intended for stationary de-vices are deployed on mobile ones.

Another concern is how these generic solutions deal with user movement across network segments. Because mobility was never con-sidered when most networks were originally designed, additional in-formation is required at the protocol layer. This additional overhead can further reduce overall performance and provide less than optimal throughput over wireless connections.

Mobile and remote users can experience poor performance when they try to adopt technologies that were implemented for stationary systems. NetMotion Mobility helps the existing network protocol im-plementations deal with the vagaries of mobile networking. It facili-tates the operation over intermittent or bandwidth-challenged links by sharing historical information, such as network latency and roundtrip time, among all transport-level sessions. This sharing of information, along with other advanced algorithms, works to reduce the transmis-sion of "gratuitous" data. In the end, transmission times can be re-duced, because less data is being sent. This saves valuable time, en-hances the user's experience, and can increase the network's performance.

UNDERSTANDING APPLICATION PERSISTENCE

Because users with wireless devices are not tethered to a fixed inter-connect, they can unwittingly move out of a coverage area. They may also choose to suspend operations to extend battery life. Such normal communication interruptions can wreak havoc with existing transport protocol implementations and cause user applications to either lock up or terminate.

To minimize such interruptions, most wireless solutions require customizing both the applications and the network. As a result, most current solutions are limited in scope and restricted to a specific set of applications. Critical applications are still relegated to stationary or desktop systems. When a company tries to deploy these applications to their mobile devices, mobile users spend a lot of time getting back on the network after losing their connections. They must log in again, reauthenticate, possibly navigate through multiple screens to find the point where they left off, and then reenter any lost data. In the end, users become frustrated and feel unproductive. This irritation can cost your company precious time and money.

Intermittent network connectivity can wreak havoc on mobile applications for many reasons. But solutions from several providers ensure that network application sessions are not terminated even when a mobile device suspends operation, a user disconnects or removes the wireless modem from the mobile device, or a device temporarily moves out of the coverage area.

Various products maintain the state of each user's applications on the network when the mobile device is out of coverage, or has been suspended to prolong battery life. Once back in contact with the network, the applications seamlessly resume where they left off.

PLANNING FOR ROAMING ISSUES

Over the past several years, network installations have been segmented for management and security reasons. To aid network segmentation deployment, the networking industry has worked hard to allow dynamic configuration of systems when they attach to a particular segment. However, once application sessions are established over existing protocols, the network assumes that a device remains attached to that segment for the duration of the session. But mobile devices can wander to different areas and the communications pipe can be easily broken. To avoid this, companies have had to either redesign their network interconnections or customize their applications, both of which cost time and money.

Wandering out of range or between network segments confuses applications and protocol stacks. Most wireless users today feel that they are using "bleeding edge" technology, so they accept frequent disruptions in service because they seem to be a fact of life. NetMotion Mobility's advanced roaming algorithms allow users to roam without disconnecting—not just from one network interconnect to another, but across network segments, and even to different networks altogether. If a mobile device is equipped with more than one wireless card, NetMotion Mobility automatically switches to the card that offers the highest bandwidth (see Figure 4-4).

NetMotion Mobility users do not have to restart their machines to obtain a new address and application session persistence is maintained. Using its client-server architecture, the NetMotion Mobility

Figure 4-4. NetMotion Mobility enables a default setting to the highest available bandwidth.

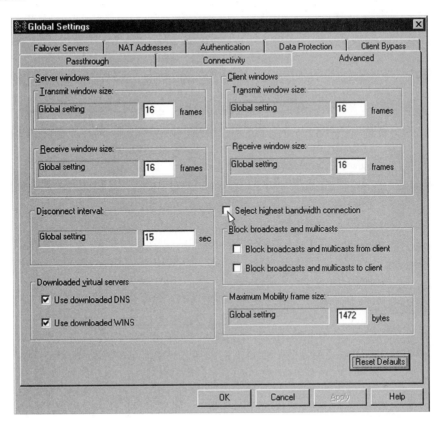

server maintains the state of each mobile device and handles the complex session management required for continuous connections to the network-based applications. When a mobile device becomes unreachable because it suspends operation, moves out of coverage, or changes its current point of presence address (roaming), the server maintains the connection to the network peer by acknowledging receipt of data and queuing requests. Once the mobile node and the NetMotion server are in contact again, the state of each connection is resynchronized, thus providing continuous network computing.

OFF-THE-SHELF EQUIPMENT INTEGRATION

Most companies do not own the source code for applications that they use to access critical information, especially the networking components. They either purchase canned applications or libraries that enable access to the stored information. If the latter is the case, these libraries (in binary form) are then linked in to customized front-end applications. These off-the-shelf applications may suffer from the mobility problems mentioned above. To recustomize each important application for mobile deployment strains the IT department's resources and increases the time and cost of deployment.

NetMotion Mobility replaces no standard operating system components and can be deployed on any standard wireless device using Windows 2000, Windows XP, Windows 9x, Windows CE, or Pocket PC. Users and IT professionals have familiar and existing interfaces and tools to work with. Using these familiar interfaces reduces help desk calls because there is little or no learning curve.

In most cases, customizing an application for mobile use is not a viable solution, especially when the company does not own the code. With NetMotion Mobility, there is no need to modify or recompile internally developed or off-the-shelf applications to give wireless users access to enterprise resources. The same applications users find valuable at their desktops can be easily deployed, as long as there are no applicable policy or bandwidth requirement limitations. In general, if there is a way to forward IP datagrams between the corresponding nodes, NetMotion and the off-the-shelf application can be seamlessly deployed. With NetMotion Mobility's compression and performance enhancing algorithms, the performance of the application may even increase

MANAGEMENT AND CONTROL ISSUES

Many wireless WANs work by connecting different buildings and company divisions. Because there is no specific central point but a collection of wireless LANs, technical and real-people turf battles can rage over who controls access to the network. These disputes can result in different policies for different divisions. The outcome can be chaotic.

Because the NetMotion Mobility Server is aware of every session that mobile devices establish, IT managers can determine the status of each individual device from one location. NetMotion Mobility management and administration services include applying policies at a user or group level, statistical tracking of behaviors on the system, traffic studies, and system troubleshooting.

Because it uses these standard components and operates only on the application's data, NetMotion Mobility seamlessly and securely operates over and through existing policy-enforcing equipment such as firewalls.

WHAT YOU HAVE LEARNED

Wireless Wide Area Networks, or Wireless WANs can bridge branch offices of a company, cover a much more extensive area than wireless LANs. Unlike wireless LANs, which are generally used on an office floor or within a building, a building or limited wireless WANs can cover entire office complexes, college campuses, or even distant points within a metropolitan area.

Unlike wireless local area networks (WLANs), the coverage area for WWANs is normally measured in miles rather than feet.

In this chapter, you learned how to evaluate whether or not you need a Wireless WAN, how these networks function, and how to purchase equipment and design solutions that will be secure and efficient.

MOVING ON

In Chapter 5, we discuss how your wireless WAN can work with Wi-Fi to enable your traveling staff to access the Internet wirelessly, and at high speed.

GETTING YOUR LAPTOP READY FOR YOUR WIRELESS NETWORK AND THE INTERNET

The chapters in this part of the book target individuals who use Wi-Fi wireless networks at work and while traveling. After reading this chapter you will have a basic understanding of how to connect your laptop to your wireless local area network (LAN), and then to the Internet using Wi-Fi networks.

The wireless network adapter in your laptop (or desktop) computer transmits a digital signal through the access point, back and forth to the other computers in your LAN, and, in most cases, to the computers on the Internet (assuming your LAN is connected to the Internet). The wireless LAN also enables you to print to network printers and to share files with other people on your company LAN.

Although wired LANs allow you to connect to the Internet, send E-Mail, and share files and printers, a wireless LAN can facilitate all these activities from locations where wired network jacks do not exist.

In some cases, a wireless LAN can even save your company a good deal of money by making it unnecessary to install network cable to every location that requires network access. For example, if you have a laptop, a wireless LAN enables you to carry it, as well as its network, Internet, and printer connections around your office without ever losing a signal and without ever connecting a cable to the wall.

Wi-Fi-compatible equipment complies with the Institute of Electrical and Electronic Engineers (IEEE) 802.11b, 802.11a and new, 54 kilobit-per-second 802.11g standards. You may see wireless LAN products that advertise compatibility with any of these standards, but the Wi-Fi logo (see Figure 5-1) means that the product has passed a number of tests that determine whether the product can work with similar products from other vendors. Odd as it may seem, 802.11a products are not interoperable with 802.11b or 802.11g products. Admittedly, 802.11a is a faster standard than traditionally 11 megabit-per-second 802.11b, but there are only a few 802.11a products on the market. On the other hand, Wi-Fi 802.11b and, increasingly, 802.11g, products are widely available.

Whenever you use your computer at work, you should rarely have to think about the wired network that connects your computer to printers, file servers, E-Mail, and the Internet—except, of course, if the network goes down. When you use a wireless LAN, however, you should know whether you have a good connection before you use the network. You need to understand a few basics about the equipment so you can

Figure 5-1. To ensure wireless network capability, look for the Wi-Fi logo on wireless network equipment.

tell if it is working. Otherwise, wired LANs and wireless LANs are essentially the same, except that wireless LANs use radios to make their connections.

For the remainder of this chapter, unless stated otherwise, everything covered applies to Wi-Fi products as well as to other related products that follow.

MEET YOUR WIRELESS STATION

Wireless networking involves at least two radios. The computer or device that you use to connect to the wireless LAN is called a station or client. Most often, a WLAN station is a personal computer that contains a wireless network adapter, enabling the computer to communicate wirelessly with the LAN. The computer that your station talks to can be another station, but is more likely a base station, or access point, that connects your station to the larger LAN (see Figure 5-2).

If you use a desktop computer that is connected to a wireless LAN, the adapter inside the computer may, in fact, be a hardware adapter that enables the use of the PC card adapter in the desktop. With this type of adapter, you can also remove the PC card (in many products, you must first turn off your computer) and use it in a laptop computer. However, wireless network adapters for desktop computers in which the radio is permanently mounted on the circuit board are becoming increasingly available. You will recognize these wireless products by their 4-inch antenna attached to the back.

Access Points

In an office setting, the heart of the wireless LAN is a device called an Access Point (see Figure 5-3). Apple calls its version of the device a base station, but most manufacturers use the term access point. Regardless of terminology, both refer to a device that communicates with wireless stations and connects these stations to the LAN. In many companies, access points are mounted on the wall or, as improbable as it may sound, even on the ceiling. Because each access point contains a

Figure 5-2. The Belkin Wireless Network Access Point connects to a wired LAN.

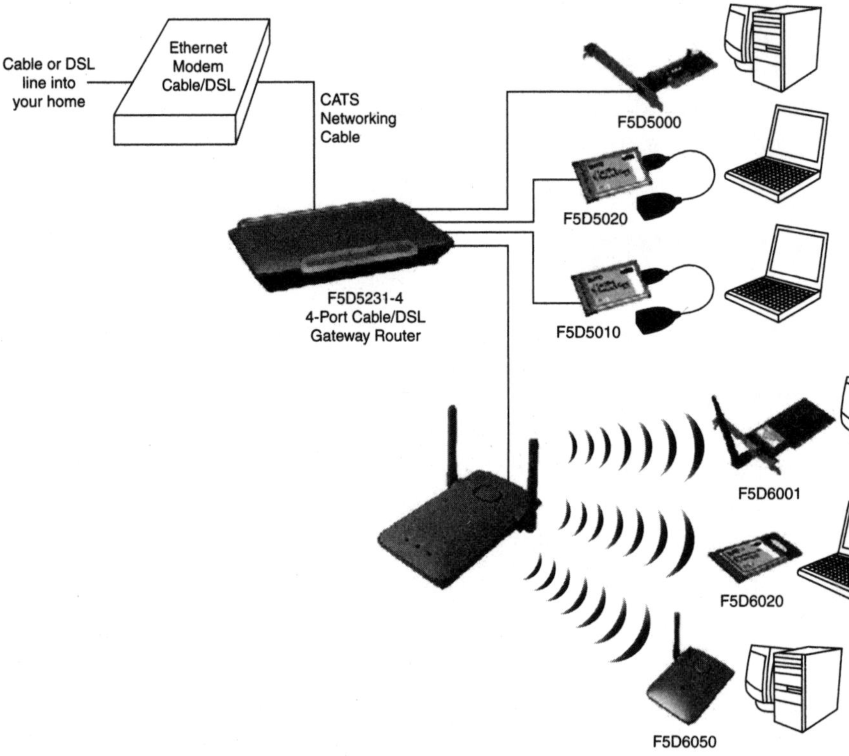

Cable or DSL line into your home

Ethernet Modem Cable/DSL

CATS Networking Cable

F5D5000

F5D5020

F5D5010

F5D5231-4 4-Port Cable/DSL Gateway Router

F5D6001

F5D6020

F5D6050

Figure 5-3. The SymbolAP 3021 is another popular Access Point.

radio, the AP should typically be mounted in a location that allows it to send and receive signals with the least amount of obstruction.

Each access point allows your network administrator to manage several parameters that enable each station to communicate with the access point and the LAN. These parameters include the following:

- The name of the wireless network.

- The channel on which the access point is broadcasting. There are multiple radio channels available for use by wireless networks.

- The wired equivalent privacy (WEP) encryption key, which protects the data sent over the WLAN from eavesdropping.

- To ensure successful communication between the access point and the station, the network name (sometimes called the SSm) in your station must be set to the same value as the network name setting in the access point. Similarly, the WEP key in your station must be set to the same value as the WEP key setting in the access point. The radio in your wireless network adapter will automatically find the right channel.

CONNECTING TO THE WIRELESS LAN

When connecting to the wireless LAN, you should not have to do much more than insert a wireless network PC card into the computer's PC card. If the signal is too weak, the radio will first try transmitting at slower speeds. Eventually, your wireless network adapter will disconnect itself from the LAN if it cannot reestablish an adequate signal. Often, shifting the position of your computer can change the strength of the signal it receives. Ultimately, you may have to move closer to the access point or to a different location with a stronger signal.

Every Wi-Fi hardware manufacturer provides a software configuration utility that enables you to check signal strength easily. Most of these utilities are designed to run only on Windows. If you are using Windows XP, you can use built-in Windows XP software to check the signal.

The following section details the steps you should take to display signal strength information on Windows computers.

A CHIP ON YOUR WIRELESS NETWORK

A significant factor driving the rapid expansion of Wi-Fi–certified products is the existence of two high-quality radio chipsets (from Intersil and Lucent) that implement the IEEE 802.11b/Wi-Fi standard. One of these two chipsets is found in the majority of IEEE 802.11b access point and wireless network adapters available for sale.

Intersil's Wi-Fi–certified PRISM II chipset is clearly the most popular among wireless networking hardware manufacturers. Intersil also has a newer, more highly integrated PRISM 2.5 chipset (see Figure 5-4). Manufacturers who use one of the PRISM chipsets include 3Com, Compaq (WLI00), GemTek, Addtron D-Link, Intel, BrQffiM, and LeMerv Solutions.

Figure 5-4. Intersil's Wi-Fi–certified chipsets are found in many wireless-enabled devices.

Figure 5-5. Wireless chipsets such as this provide the processing power for wireless PCI cards in many notebook computers.

Lucent Technology's chipset is found on products by such companies as IstWave, IBM, Agere ORiNOCO, Dell (1150), Toshiba Artem, ELSA, Sony, Enterasys, Buffalo, and Hewlett Packard. Broadcom's new chipset is found in the wireless-network enabled Dell TrueMobile 1300 wireless mini PCI card (see Figure 5-5).

USING Wi-Fi WITH WINDOWS 95, 98, Me, NT, AND 2000

Not all Wi-Fi equipment manufacturers use the same software to configure and test wireless network adapters but most use one of two varieties: Lucent or Intersil. Look for the icon that appears in the Windows Quick Launch toolbar if you are using a wireless LAN PC card designed by Lucent, and either Windows 95, 98, Me, NT, or 2000 as the operating system. Note that the icon is a miniature bar graph. When all five bars in the graph are green, your wireless LAN radio is getting an excellent signal. As the signal gets weaker, the number of green bars decreases until the entire graph turns yellow or goes blank, indicating a poor or nonexistent signal. You can also move the mouse over the icon to see a message balloon that indicates an excellent, good, fair, or poor signal.

If you are using wireless network hardware that is based on the Intersil Ird chipset, an icon that looks like a small computer appears in the Windows taskbar. When the signal is adequate, you will see a green screen. When the signal is weak, the screen in the icon turns yellow. If it is too weak to receive information, the screen turns red.

USING Wi-Fi WITH WINDOWS XP

Windows XP is the first version of Windows that comes with built-in support for wireless LANs in general and built-in drivers for some Wi-Fi equipment. A bit of configuration is still required when the wireless network adapter card is first installed in your computer, but it is not necessary to install any software from the manufacturer of the wireless network adapter.

After you have inserted the wireless network adapter and started the computer, Windows XP displays a network connection icon, in the notification area of the Windows XP taskbar. You can move your mouse over this icon to display the signal strength message.

You may wish to see a signal strength bar graph instead. To display this feature, perform the following steps:

1. Right-click a network connection icon (there can be more than one if you have more than one network adapter in your computer) in the notification area of the taskbar at the bottom of the screen to display a pop-up menu.

2. Click the Status option. Windows XP displays the wireless network connection status dialog box. This dialog contains a signal strength bar graph on the right side.

3. To close the window, click "Close."

ACCESSING THE INTERNET OVER A PUBLIC WIRELESS NETWORK

This section targets individuals who will be using Wi-Fi wireless networks and helps users get connected to public wireless networks that are available in places such as coffee shops, hotels, and airports.

PUBLIC WIRELESS LANs

As of the publication date of this book, Wi-Fi technology has produced two types of public wireless networks used to access the Internet. These technologies are:

Commercial wireless LAN Internet service providers. Public wireless LANs of this type provide Internet connectivity for a fee in public places such as coffee shops and airports, as well as hotels, locations sometimes called wireless hot spots.

Community wireless networks. Several communities in the United States have collaborated to set up a wireless network that connects enrolled members of the neighborhood free-of-charge.

LEARNING ABOUT COMMERCIAL Wi-Fi ACCESS PROVIDERS

Fortunately, high-speed Internet connections are becoming more common in the major hotel chains frequented by business travelers, and even in a few of the smaller nationwide hotel chains such as Summerfield Suites, Fairfield Inn, Hampton Inn, Comfort Inn, and Courtyard by Marriott. The typical hotel-based high-speed connection requires that your laptop have an Ethernet port and that you pay about $9.95 for 24 hours of service.

The availability of a high-speed connection in your hotel room is convenient, however, it only gives you connectivity in a single location. If you are attending a conference in the hotel, it would be much more convenient if you could access the Internet and download company E-Mail from anywhere in the building.

WAYPORT

Wayport, Inc. (*www.Wayport.com*), based in Austin, Texas, is one of the leading providers of high-speed Internet connections in hotels.

Wayport provides high-speed Internet access in more than 525 hotels, airports, and conference centers across the United States at
speeds up to fifty to two hundred times faster than traditional dial-up
modem services. Wayport also serves several locations in Europe
(see Figure 5-6).

Wayport has been providing wired Ethernet Internet connections
to customers worldwide in a growing number of hotels and
other public venues since 1997. In the last year, Wayport has extended its service to Wi-Fi wireless equipment users. Wayport has
started to set up major U.S. airports and hotels for all-wireless LAN
connectivity.

Wayport charges for connectivity on a daily, pay-as-you-go basis,
providing user connectivity from one of their properties for up to 24
hours a day (usually until midnight) or on a monthly basis. Travelers
can use Wayport's wireless Internet services by signing up on the spot
and paying by credit card for service until midnight. Frequent travel-

Figure 5-6. Wayport's wireless Internet service is available in several European
hotels.

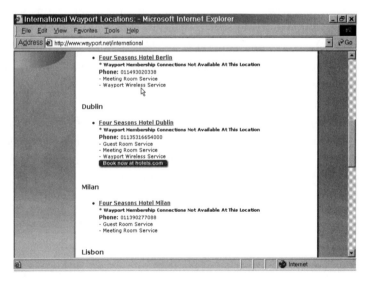

ers can apply for a set monthly rate that is based on volume of users, or for a yearly individual membership.

Wayport also offers a prepaid plan. This plan, designed for less frequent users, is similar to a phone card. Members establish an account by prepaying a set amount. They can then connect at any Wayport hotel or all-wireless airport.

Several wireless LAN hardware manufacturers have partnered with WayPort to introduce potential customers to the service by providing coupons to users for a free day of access. As part of a test project cosponsored by Wayport and Microsoft, users of Windows XP and Wi-Fi wireless LAN equipment benefited from free wireless Internet service in participating hotel lobbies and throughout all gates and terminals at Wayport's contracted air terminals. The first of these to sign on were at Dallas–Fort Worth, San Jose, Seattle–Tacoma, and Austin–Bergstrom International airports. Participating hotels include many Sheratons, Marriotts, Westins, Radissons, Doubletrees, Embassy Suites, Four Seasons, and Wyndham.

T-Mobile HotSpot is another such provider. It has "hot spots" in airports, hotels, conference centers, restaurants, coffee houses, and other public places in the United States. It has partnered with Starbucks to provide broadband wireless Internet access in several hundred of the Starbucks coffeehouses across the country (see Figure 5-7).

Similar to Wayport, T-Mobile HotSpot offers several subscription options. These include pay as you go, prepaid cards, and a high amount of unlimited usage for a year-long contract and payment of a flat monthly fee.

Wireless connectivity from T-Mobile HotSpot, Wayport, and other public wireless LAN service providers is also marketed through wireless LAN service aggregators. A wireless LAN aggregator offers regional or nationwide subscriptions that provide access to wireless networks that may be maintained by many different vendors. Boingo Wireless, which was started by the founders of the popular EarthLink Internet access service, offers subscriptions that include access to thousands of hot spots around the nation.

Figure 5-7. A LAN with your latte? T-Mobile HotSpots are available at Starbucks Coffee locations in numerous metro areas.

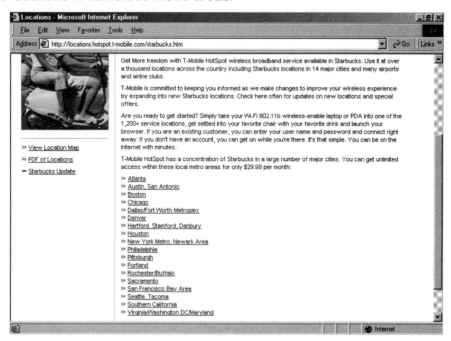

USING Wi-Fi TO ACCESS A PUBLIC WIRELESS LAN SERVICE

The following sections walk you through logging on and logging off using Wayport and T-Mobile HotSpot as examples to give you an idea how to operate public wireless LAN services.

When connecting to the Internet from a wireless Starbucks store, perform the following steps:

1. Turn off encryption.

2. Set this configuration to renew the Internet provider address when selected: when you sign on to T-Mobile HotSpot, the service will assign a new Internet provider address to your computer for use while connected to the service.

3. When you save this configuration, your wireless client/station software should be able to detect the signal from the T-Mobile HotSpot network. If your client software does not "see" the T-Mobile HotSpot network, check the first two steps to make sure you entered the correct information.

4. Open your Web browser.

5. Either enter a promotion code for any special offer that you may have obtained from a wireless LAN equipment manufacturer, or click the sign up button to go to the screen where you can choose one of the T-Mobile HotSpot payment options (see Figure 5-8). This screen consists of two windows: a small window hovering over a larger window. When you use the large window to browse the Internet, the small window will seem to disappear. But do not forget that it is still open in the background. You will use the small window to log off.

Figure 5-8. Signing up for the WayPort Wi-Fi service on WayPort's Web site.

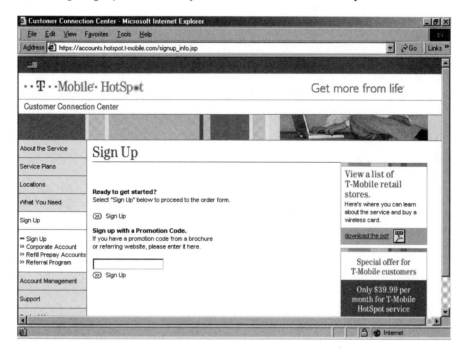

6. If you want to see the status of your T-Mobile HotSpot account or make changes in your account, click the account management link. Otherwise, from this point, you can use your Web browser to navigate the Internet as you always do, keeping in mind that you are using up your T-Mobile HotSpot minutes.

7. When you have finished using the Internet connection, find the small window (which should still be open) and click the LogOff T-Mobile HotSpot link. T-Mobile HotSpot closes the window and stops charging your account for access.

USING Wi-Fi AT AIRPORTS AND HOTELS

Wayport is the service provider in many airports and in more than four hundred hotels. If you find that you need to connect via Wayport, follow these steps:

1. Using the configuration program for your Wi-Fi–equipped notebook computer, sign on to Wayport. The service will assign a new Internet provider address to your computer for use while connected to the service (see Figure 5-9).

2. When you save this configuration, your wireless client/station software should be able to detect the signal from the Wayport network.

Figure 5-9. Signing on to WayPort from a Wi-Fi enabled notebook PC.

3. Open your Web browser. When it attempts to open your default home page, Wayport displays a screen.

4. If you have already established an account, click "Use Wayport Membership" to display the sign-on screen. Otherwise, either click "Purchase a Connection" or "Use a Coupon," depending on whether you have a promotional coupon.

5. Click "Go to Requested Web site" to begin browsing the Internet.

6. When you are finished, simply close the Web browser.

COMMUNITY WIRELESS LANs

Someone has to pay for the Internet service for community wireless LANs. Ideally, the community finds a sponsor, but more typically, several members of the community share the cost of the high-speed Internet connection, as well as the cost of transmitting the signal.

These services generally go by the name of WISP, which stands for wireless Internet service provider. In the majority of cases, these services are free. Most metropolitan areas have several. You can find a list at http://thelist.internet.com/.

Most WISPs have similar connection procedures. Personal Telco in Portland, Oregon, is typical. Its set-up and sign-on procedures are typical, and are cited here for illustrative example purposes.

To sign on to a WISP using your wireless LAN-capable laptop computer, perform the following steps:

1. Make sure that your computer is ready to connect to an access point (the same as it would be to use the wireless at home or work).

2. Set your extended set service ID (ESSID) to your WISP's Web address. The ESSID is usually accessed through the set-up menu on your notebook.

3. Come within range of the node. You may be able to plan for this step in advance by checking the Web site of the WISP you plan to use. If you have not had time to do this, try using a Wireless Sniffer. This is software you can download to and install on your notebook computer in advance of your Wi-Fi session. Once you do this, you can use the Sniffer to find a Wi-Fi service in your area. A list of wireless sniffing software is provided on many WISP Web sites. Personal Telco's list, which is fairly comprehensive, can be found at *http://www.personaltelco.net/ index.cgi/WirelessSniffer* (see Figure 5-10).

4. Once you are in range of a WISP, make sure your computer can connect via Wi-Fi. On Windows, this can be done by clicking

Figure 5-10. A list of "wireless sniffers," as provided on the Personal Telco Project Web site. Courtesy, Personal Telco.

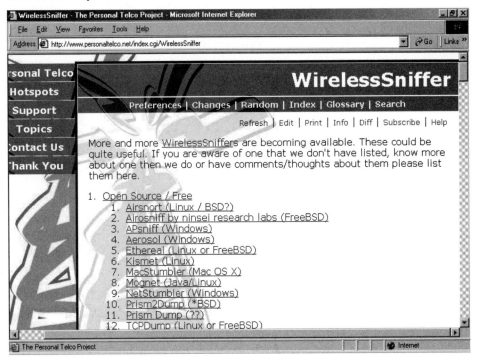

"Start," then "Run," and typing "winipcfg." Be sure to select your wireless card in the drop-down box.

5. Open a web browser and try and go somewhere. Often, you will be routed to the Web page of the WISP you are using.

6. Read the terms and conditions, if you accept them click "I Agree . . ." to continue and get access.

7. Once you are "on," just use the Internet and the Web as you please.

WHAT YOU HAVE LEARNED

In this chapter, you learned about the equipment necessary to connect your laptop to your wireless LAN, as well as to the Internet. You explored the worlds of wireless stations, chipsets, and Access Points. Hopefully, you are familiar enough with the basics to evaluate this equipment for purchase, and connect to it once your wireless network is built.

In the second half of this chapter, you learned about how you can take your wireless-enabled notebook computer on the road with you, and what commercial and free services are available that will let you do this quickly and with a minimum of technical hassle.

CHAPTER 6

HOW YOUR BUSINESS CAN USE WIRELESS NETWORKING

Wireless networking can help your business in innumerable ways. This technology can help you gather information from varied sources and then route it to one location. It can help you with training, inventory control, manufacturing management, and customer service. Should you have an older building without the power infrastructure in place to tie all your computers and computing equipment into a networked environment, wireless networking can help there as well.

In the workplace, wireless local area networks (LANs) are often used to supplement rather than replace standard wired networks. Frequently, they are used within an office to provide the final few feet of connectivity between a mobile user and the backbone network. An example of this could be a group of employees taking their wireless LAN-capable notebooks into a conference room. The notebook computers could then be used to send notes taken during the meeting to the access point that ties the wireless signals together with the wireless network.

Among the more widespread applications, retailers such as Sears and Wal-Mart are using wireless handheld devices to check inventory, maintain a supply of items on the shelves, make price changes, and order additional merchandise when needed. These and many other retailers do this by equipping handheld devices to tie in to their networks, and then from there, to their databases where the relevant information is housed.

In this chapter, we look at some real-life ways that businesses and educational institutions are using wireless networking to better foster the flow of information and ideas.

LEARNING ABOUT REAL-WORLD WIRELESS NETWORKING APPLICATIONS

The Sugarcreek Local School District in Bellbrook, Ohio, formed an eight-person strategic planning committee to set goals for the district to enter the twenty-first century. Comprising four individuals from the community and four from the school system, this committee challenged the school district with putting a twenty-five-workstation computer laboratory in every school building, and a computer in every classroom. At nearly the same time, the Ohio State Legislature mandated the Ohio State Board of Education to develop and implement a statewide Education Management Information System (EMIS).

Ohio's EMIS mandate requires the periodic downloading of school district census and financial information, as well as student and staff demographics, attendance, performance, and course information. The State established a network of designated data acquisition sites (A-sites) to serve as validation and aggregation points. Communicating with the A-site had previously been accomplished through a dumb terminal linked to the Miami Valley Educational Computer Association (MVECA) via a 2,400-baud modem. Having computers in every building and having them all connected through a network would certainly facilitate the gathering and compiling of this information. Networking every school building in the district to its own information server could also provide each classroom, teacher, and student with access to the latest educational programs and data. It became obvious that a computer network connecting all buildings in the school district should be a high-priority item.

Armed with these requirements, the committee began the process of soliciting proposals and quotations for equipment and installation of such a network. After bids in the $1.8 to 2 million range were received, the project stalled and was put on the shelf. Two years later the superintendent got the ball rolling again by asking what it would take to get the computers from the original project in place over the next two years.

A revised plan called for a two-phase approach to installing all the computers. The first phase consisted of installing a computer in each high school classroom and a twenty- to thirty-terminal laboratory in each of the four buildings. The budget for this phase was $125,000 with some funding being available from the State and some from private/corporate donations. In the second phase the goal was fulfilled, with a PC in every classroom in the district and in each of the administration offices.

Next came the question of networking these computers. How would they communicate with the other buildings? Several methods were considered. To set up and operate a T1 phone line with a speed of 1.54 megabits per second would cost $20,000 for the first year. In addition, there would be an annual recurring cost of approximately $10,000. To set up and operate a then-current technology wireless system would cost approximately $40,000. This system would have a maximum distance of 2.5 miles, which would not be a problem for this network application. However, a speed of only 64 kilobits per second would greatly handicap the usefulness of the network.

C-SPEC Corporation, a local area company specializing in total network solutions, was called in to work on the concept. They had been working on a prototype wireless LAN, based on spread-spectrum technology that was highly reliable, capable of ranges of up to twenty miles, and could transmit at the faster speed of 2 megabits per second. The Sugarcreek Local School District became the pilot project for C-SPEC to design, build, and install the OverLAN® Wireless Bridge/IP Router. One of the few stipulations called for packetized information, which could be achieved with AppleTalk, Novell, or an Intel Proshare card.

According to the district, this project was very successful and has been in place, running almost flawlessly, for more than three years now. The cost to set up and operate this wireless system for the first year was just under $16,000 and there is no recurring annual cost. The system currently connects all five buildings in the district.

The network ties together 650 computers on six servers (see Figure 6-1). The current capabilities of this network include multimedia, Internet, and videoconferencing, in addition to providing the flow of information to and from the classrooms, building offices, and the central offices. This system is used by the administration to access the various files needed in compiling the EMIS reports.

At first, students using classroom terminals accessed information from the Greene County Public Library through a network connection to the T1 line that provides the link to MVECA. The Greene County Public Library applied for a grant from the State to tie its Bellbrook branch directly into the school's network with an OverLAN® Wireless

Figure 6-1. On its wireless network, the Sugarcreek School District has tied 650 computers together.

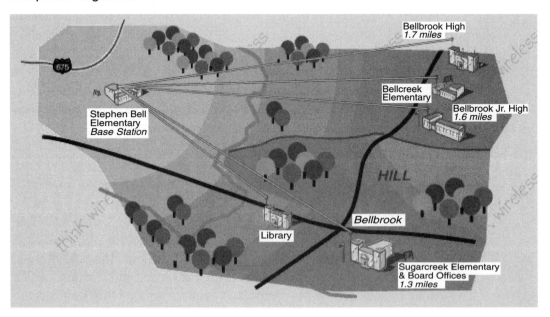

Bridge. The library became the sixth building in the system, and is now accessed directly through the wireless network.

Educational programs and data available to every classroom could also be made available to any person who has access to the Internet. Students would be able to access their own lessons, get special tutoring, or participate in individual study programs from home.

OCEAN SPRAY: CRANBERRY JUICE MANUFACTURER IMPLEMENTS A WIRELESS LAN

Ocean Spray's Kenosha, Wisconsin, warehouse is one of six regional manufacturing/warehousing distribution facilities for Ocean Spray. While each produces juice from locally grown fruit, all facilities distribute the full Ocean Spray product line in their region. That requires considerable interwarehouse shipments.

Prior to adopting a wireless LAN technology at the Kenosha warehouse, two people were dedicated to walking around the 300,000 square foot warehouse just to find open storage locations for incoming pallet loads. When it was time to pick cases of the company's juice products, workers had trouble reading the pallet case markings. Tracking of shipments by customers required many hours to review paperwork and determine who received which products from which lots.

When the managers of the Ocean Spray Kenosha warehouse faced an increase of 15 percent in case volume and a 10 percent increase in SKU count, it was time to make a change in their inventory information management system. They decided on a wireless system, and today, every lift truck in the Kenosha warehouse is outfitted with a radio frequency data communication (RFDC) terminal. All storage locations are bar-coded, as is every pallet load. A warehouse management system (WMS) coordinates activities, from receiving through shipping of finished goods. To maximize efficiencies, the server that the WMS systems runs on at Kenosha is fully integrated with the

Figure 6-2. Bar-code scanners such as the Symbol PDT-6100 can transmit inventory data over a wireless network.

mainframe at Ocean Spray's corporate headquarters in Middleboro, Massachusetts.

The intent in this application, as well as numerous others throughout North American manufacturing and retail establishments, is to make the data in the users' corporate system as current as the last bar code scanned on the floor (see Figure 6-2).

With the new system, pallet loads arriving from another warehouse have a bar-coded pallet label, including the product identification number, product code date or expiration date, the plant of manufacture, line of manufacture, and a sequentially assigned serial number. A lift truck operator scans the label in receiving. The RF terminal sends that data to the warehouse software, which immediately designates a storage location and relays it back to the RF terminal on the lift truck. Every storage location is identified by a bar-code label either suspended from the ceiling for floor locations or attached to a rack face. The operator scans that bar code to confirm offloading in the correct location.

At headquarters, the mainframe receives orders by Ocean Spray's electronic data interchange (EDI) network. It then releases orders to locations. At Kenosha, the WMS manages order picking, balances work loads, and selects pick sequences for lift truck operators. The dock control module then releases orders for picking.

Each line item and quantity required appear on the designated lift truck's RFDC terminal. To confirm accuracy, the operator scans the bar code label on the full pallet or at the rack location for less than full pallet picks. The RF terminal directs the operator to the designated dock door for immediate loading on an over-the-road trailer, all under the control of the warehouse software. Using the inventory data captured by the RF terminals, the WMS automatically generates the pack list and bill of lading for each over-the-road trailer. Confirmations of line items picked and shipped are then sent to the mainframe for invoicing.

PRODUCTIVITY GAINS

The results of the wireless technology have been beneficial, and more precisely, statistically quantifiable. Beyond eliminating the original inefficiencies, the automatic data collection (ADC) system allowed Kenosha to ship an additional 1.8 million cases of the product in 2,200 fewer worker hours during the first year. Hourly productivity increased from 451 to 550 cases handled per worker. In addition, inventory accuracy now exceeds 98 percent, and inventory turns increased as inventory levels fell by 121,000 cases. Ocean Spray says the new system provides a standard 100 percent lot traceability by customer, within minutes.

The wireless system was initially installed in the Kenosha, Wisconsin, warehouse and is now in the process of being installed at Ocean Spray's other manufacturing/warehousing locations around the country.

WIRELESS GIVES A CHIROPRACTIC CLINIC "BACKBONE"

The challenge to do more with less is driving primary providers throughout the health care industry to look for more efficient ways to run their practices. As administrative burdens rise and reimbursement rates decline, every provider is asking the same question: How can they lower operating expenses, increase the number of patient visits, and make care faster and more convenient? And how can they accomplish those objectives with a rapid financial return on investment and little or no added system support? Northwest Health, a small naturopathic and chiropractic clinic in Chicago, Illinois, is one provider that has found answers to those questions.

The goal was to connect pen-based mobile computers to the wired network in the central office. The pen-based devices are used by the clinic's two doctors, who see patients in six separate treating rooms. As they visit each patient, they record what they call S.O.A.P., or subjective, objective, assessment, and plan notes.

Before Northwest installed its wireless LAN, doctors had access to patient records only through the PCs in its front office. Now, with wireless-adapted, pen-based mobile computers and commercially available S.O.A.P. software (see Figure 6-3) not only can Northwest's partners access patient records from any room in the office, they can enter notes on the spot as they provide care. Setting up the wireless LAN and connecting it to the existing Ethernet network was easy: the partners did it themselves in about two hours.

Figure 6-3. Pen-based mobile computers are used by hospitals to record patient information. The information is then sent wirelessly to the patient database.

One of the partners in the practice said the main goal in setting up their wireless LAN was to speed up the caregiving process, allowing them to see more patients as a result. Because of the information-routing capabilities of the wireless LAN, each of the two doctors at the practice says that they are able to schedule in more appointments. These account for a combined total of three to four additional patients per day. Not only is additional patient income generated but substantial amounts of money are saved.

Because doctors at Northwest Health now have mobile access to patient records as they go from room to room providing treatment, they never have to go back to a computer on the wired network, and no one has to transcribe or dictate notes for entry into a computer in the front office. By freeing the documentation process from paper and desktop computers, the wireless system eliminated the need for at least one part-time employee at the front desk dedicated to transcription. That saved at least $10,000 to $12,000 per year, which allowed the system to pay for itself in less than a year. An additional benefit of the notes generated through the S.O.A.P. software is better documentation for insurance billing and letters to attorneys in legal cases.

The wireless network also gives doctors access to information that they otherwise would not have access to while with a patient. Because the network gives doctors access to all of the network's services, such as printing, the practitioners at Northwest Health can print a patient note or schedule an appointment and send that information wirelessly to their front office. They can even access a patient's record, enter a treatment plan, and enter the financial transaction directly. The information goes right into the hard drive on their file server, which is backed up every night.

JET ENGINE MANUFACTURER TAKES OFF WITH WIRELESS WAN

Pratt & Whitney is a leading jet engine manufacturer with widespread international operations. The company also has a major aftermarket business for jet engine parts. Think aftermarket, and the mission-critical need for rapid and highly efficient inventory control comes immediately to mind. The company runs this business out of forty facilities around the world.

The company also says that when they manufacture a jet engine, they need to record each part number they place into it. When their outside suppliers make metal forgings in a long bar, for instance, they need to know where the bar came from, as well as all actions taken with that specific bar during its entire service life.

Pratt & Whitney decided to investigate wireless networking as a solution to process this information more efficiently. In a joint venture with Singapore Airlines, it launched a network with six Intermec, Inc. wireless access points across four warehouse locations, and twelve wireless mobile computers with integrated bar code scanning capabilities. The goal was to assemble information and then transfer it via a software interface into a corporate database.

The old way involved going to the appropriate box where the records for the item were kept, pulling the paperwork out, entering the information from the paperwork into a terminal, and then returning the paperwork to the box.

In day-to-day operation, workers in the Singapore facility use their wireless mobile computers to scan bar codes or enter information via keypad for such transactions as goods receipt, put-away, pick, bin transfers, or to generate bar code labels. The device then wirelessly passes the information to one of six access points, where it enters the company's local area network, feeds into Pratt & Whitney's wide area network (WAN), and is ultimately passed into the company's single SAP server which is made by German-based enterprise systems solutions giant SAP AG. Once the data are part of SAP, the whereabouts of every box, part, and bin is visible to Pratt & Whitney facilities worldwide.

Pratt & Whitney has now implemented this wireless technology in a total of five New England locations. Company representatives happily report significantly more efficient inventory and parts control operations.

WHAT YOU HAVE LEARNED

The primary purpose of this chapter is to show you that wireless networking is not just an avocation for geeks. Far from it. There are numerous examples in the manufacturing, educational, retail and health care sectors. That's just for starters.

Reading about these real-life success stories has hopefully energized you for the specific surveying, equipment evaluation, construction, and training tasks that will be ahead of you. These issues are discussed in the following chapters.

CHAPTER 7

BUYING AND INSTALLING WIRELESS NETWORKING EQUIPMENT

In the previous chapters, you learned the basics of wireless networking. In this chapter, you will learn what specific equipment you will need, what this equipment will cost, and how to shop for it.

SHOPPING FOR WIRELESS LAN EQUIPMENT

A good bit of your equipment acquisition strategy will depend on the scope of the wireless local area network (LAN) you are planning, as well as whether the wireless LAN is going to be operated by your company or at least within a corporate setting.

Here are some products you will need for your wireless LAN:

- A network interface card (NIC).

- A universal serial bus (USB) adapter, especially if a NIC card is not practical.

- One or more Access Points.

- A router to connect your wireless LAN to your wired LAN and Internet connection.

- Driver software that you will use to set up and control your wireless LAN from your computer system.

SMART SHOPPING: QUESTIONS TO ASK

This equipment is available via vendor Web sites, at computer retailers, via many electronics dealers, and even some computer repair outlets. Before you shop for specific equipment, you should be prepared to ask the following questions:

- Is this particular product compatible with the computer operating system it will be installed on?

- What are my pricing options?

- How long is the product covered by the warranty?

- When does the warranty begin?

- Is there a service plan or service contract? If so, what are the terms, and what does the level of contracted service entail?

- Is the product compliant with the Institute of Electrical and Electronic Engineers (IEEE) 802.11 standard?

- Is encryption available in order to provide higher security?

- What are the limitations of the coverage?

- How should the product be returned if it becomes defective? Does the vendor provide onsite or offsite maintenance?

- What type of after-purchase vendor support do you offer?

Now it is time to go shopping. Here is a bit more about each of these technologies: what equipment you will need, how much it will cost, and how to install each of these products to make your wireless LAN hum with efficiency and speed. Note: model names and approximate prices were current when this book was published.

UNDERSTANDING NICs

You may need a NIC for your desktop computer, as well as your notebook computer or computers. If you choose the NIC route, you will need to select two separate types of cards for your desktop, and then for your notebook computers.

As with a wired network, wireless LANs require that each workstation have a NIC that connects it to the network. In the case of wireless, however, the NIC does not have an RJ-45 port. Instead, it contains a transmitter-receiver called a transceiver. This device comes bundled with a built-in antenna. In turn, the antenna sends and receives radio signals to and from other devices on the wireless LAN. For a desktop computer, you will want to select a peripheral component interconnect (PCI) NIC that plugs into an empty PCI slot inside your machine.

Some desktop computer NICs include the Linksys WMP11 ($99; *http://www.linksys.com*); the Netgear MA301 ($49; *http://www.netgear. com*), which also requires the MA401 PC Card; the SMC 2602W ($129; *http://www.smc.com*); the U.S. Robotics USR2415 ($99; *http://www.usr. com*); and the ZyXEL ZyAir PCI Adapter ($89; *http://www.zyxel.com*), which also requires the ZyAir 100 PC Card.

HOW TO INSTALL A NIC CARD

To install a NIC card on your desktop PC, you will want to perform the following steps:

1. Shut down your computer and turn off its power.

2. Remove the case from your computer.

3. Find an empty slot and take off the metal piece covering the rear of the slot.

4. Push the NIC card into the slot. Do not force the card in but insert it gently.

5. Place the case back over your PC.

6. Turn your computer back on. You should see a message telling you that your operating system has detected new hardware and is installing the drivers for it. Follow the on-screen instructions. You will probably be asked to restart your computer.

7. After you turn your computer on, check the status of your network interface card. To do so, right-click on the My Computer icon with your mouse. Select "Properties" from the menu of choices. If you click on the Device Manager tab, you should see your newly installed NIC card under the Network adapters section.

LEARNING ABOUT PCMCIA CARDS

NICs for notebook computers are somewhat of a different story. These devices use a credit-card-sized device called a PCMCIA (Personal Computer Memory Card International Association) card. PCMCIA cards fit into the PCMCIA slots of your notebook, and connect your computer to your wireless network (see Figure 7-1).

Most notebook computers come with PCMCIA cards already installed. If not, your systems engineer, or almost any computer repair

Figure 7-1. PCMCIA cards fit into the PCMCIA slots of notebook PCs.

shop can do this for you. If you need to purchase a PCMCIA card, they generally cost between $70 and $110. Better-known models are the Linksys WPC11 ($79), the Netgear MA401 ($69), the SMC 2632W ($79), the U.S. Robotics USR2410 ($82), and the ZyXEL ZyAir 100 PC Card ($109).

INSTALLING YOUR PCMCIA CARD DRIVERS

The installation process for the Linksys WPC11 is typical of PCMCIA installation procedures in general. This procedure involves installing the drivers for the card, and then installing the physical card itself.

If your notebook computer came with a PCMCIA card, the chances are very likely that the driver software has already been installed on it. If your notebook computer does not have a PCMCIA card, you may want to download and install drivers for the card you wish to purchase. Most computer technicians will thank you for having taken care of this chore ahead of time.

To install the drivers for your PCMCIA card in your notebook or desktop computer, perform the following steps:

1. Insert the setup disk into your CD-ROM drive. Unless you have deactivated the auto-run feature of Windows, the following screen should appear automatically.

2. The first tab across the top of the screen, labeled "Install," should now be highlighted.

3. Click "Install." The InstallShield Wizard screen appears.

4. A "Welcome to the InstallShield Wizard" screen appears. Click "Next."

5. A "Warranty Policy" screen appears. Click "Yes."

6. A "Choose Destination" screen appears. Click "Next."

At this point, a wireless mode screen will appear. Radio buttons in the box will ask you to choose between infrastructure mode and ad hoc mode. Choose infrastructure mode if you will be connecting your notebook computers via your access point to your wired LAN. Select ad-hoc mode if your wireless-equipped notebook will communicate directly with other wireless-equipped notebooks.

Because infrastructure mode is a more common setting for business environments, we have chosen set-up instructions for that mode.

To configure your PCMCIA card for infrastructure mode, perform the following steps:

1. If you selected infrastructure mode, an SSID (service set identifier) screen will appear (see Figure 7-2).

2. In the SSID box, you will be prompted to enter an SSID value in the box provided. The SSID may be up to thirty-two characters in length and may include any character on the keyboard. All SSID values on your wireless network must match. If you

Figure 7-2. Configuring a PCMCIA card with card software's SSID screen.

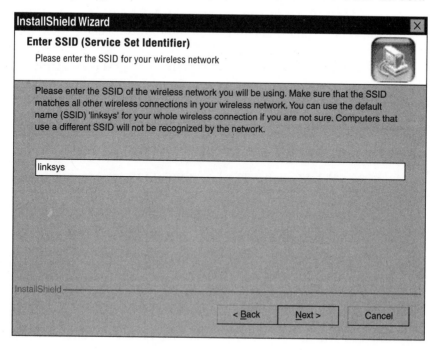

are unsure, use the default value of "linksys." Then, click the "Next" button.

2. The "Review Settings" page appears. Click "Next."

3. The "Setup Status" page appears. A moving blue bar will track the progress of the installation. After the installation is complete, a "Congratulations" box appears. In order for the drivers to be installed properly, you must restart your computer. If you choose to do it now, select "Yes, I want to restart my computer now." If you do not want to do it now, choose "No, I will restart my computer later." Once you have made your choice, click the "Finish" button to continue. Your computer will power back up, with your PCMCIA software enabled.

AN ATTRACTIVE ALTERNATIVE TO NIC

If you do not wish to risk opening your desktop computer case to install a NIC, you may want to consider a USB adapter. These devices plug directly into your USB port and may be a practical alternative to NIC cards.

If all you want to do is quickly attach a desktop computer to your wireless LAN, you will be able to do so in just a few seconds.

Available models include the Linksys WUSB11 (see Figure 7-3), the Netgear MA101, and the SMC 2662W Version 2, all of which sell for between $89 and $100.

HOW TO INSTALL YOUR USB ADAPTER

Your USB adapter is easy to install. The installation process for the Linksys WUSB11 is typical, and is used here as an example. To install your USB Adapter on your desktop computer, perform the following steps:

1. Insert the setup disk into your CD-ROM drive. The setup utility should run automatically and the screen shown below

Figure 7-3. The Linksys WUSB11 is one of the more popular USB adapters.

should appear. If it does not, click the Start button and choose Run. In the box that appears, enter D:\setup.exe (where "D" is the letter of your CD-ROM drive).

2. Click the "Install" tab on the Setup Utility box. An Install-Shield Wizard box appears. Click "Next."

3. A Warranty box will appear. Click "Yes."

4. The InstallShield Wizard box appears. This box will automatically indicate the default file where the drivers for your USB adapter will be installed on your computer. Click "Next."

5. Enter the name of your SSID for your ad hoc or infrastructure setting. The SSID must be identical for all points in the network. To join any available SSID, type "ANY." The default setting is linksys (all lowercase). Click "Next."

6. The InstallShield Wizard box appears. InstallShield Wizard will ask you to choose a wireless mode. Choose the mode that applies to your network. Ad hoc mode is used for simple peer-to-peer networking or sharing of local resources between wireless networked PCs, and infrastructure mode allows a wireless network to be integrated into an existing, wired network

through an access point, permitting roaming between access points while maintaining a connection to all network resources. Click "Next."

7. If you have selected infrastructure mode, go on to the next step. If you chose ad hoc mode, choose the correct operating channel that applies to your network. The channel you choose should be set the same as the other points in your wireless network. The default channel is set to Channel 6. Click "Next."

8. Enter in the name of your SSID for your ad hoc or infrastructure setting. The SSID must be identical for all points in the network. To join any available SSID, type "ANY." The default setting will usually be the name of the product, in this case, linksys (all lowercase). Click "Next".

9. The InstallShield Wizard will ask you to review your settings before starting to copy files. Click "Back" to review or change any settings, or select "Next" if you are satisfied with your settings.

10. The InstallShield Wizard will begin copying the files. The bar in the middle of the screen below shows the percentage of files copied. When the process is finished, you will see a "Congratulations, you have successfully installed" (or similarly worded) screen. You have now completed the installation of your Wireless USB Network.

BUYING YOUR ACCESS POINT

Access Points perform two basic functions. They can work as a wireless hub at the center of your WLAN, extending the range of your workstations. Second, they can act as a gateway for connecting your wireless LAN to a wired LAN.

Access Points typically have a transceiver with antennas, and one or more RJ-45 ports for connecting to a regular Ethernet network. Normally, you can have from two to fifteen or more workstations con-

Figure 7-4. The Linksys WAP11 Access Point enables wireless network connectivity.

nected to a single Access Point, depending on your environment and the types of speeds you expect from the network. The more Access Points you have attached to your network (such as more workstations as opposed to just a few) the slower the transmission speed of your wireless LAN will be.

Some of the more popular Access Points and their prices at the time this book was published, include the Linksys WAP11 ($99.99) (see Figure 7-4), the Netgear ME102NA ($85), the SMC 2665W ($60), and the U.S. Robotics USR2450 ($129).

HOW TO INSTALL YOUR ACCESS POINT

Before you begin using your Access Point, you will need to connect the device, install the USB drivers that come with it, and configure the driver software that will enable your Access Point to function. In this section, we cover the basic steps you will need to follow for each of these processes. Not as an endorsement, but as an acknowledgment of its popularity and its typical method of installation, we will use the Linksys WAP 11 Access Point as an illustrative example.

To connect and set up your wireless Access Point, perform the following steps:

1. Locate an optimum location for the wireless network Access Point. The best place for your wireless network Access Point is usually at the center of your wireless network, with line of sight to all of your mobile stations.

2. Fix the direction of the antenna. Try to place it in a position that can best cover your wireless network. Normally, the higher you place the antenna, the better the performance will be. The antenna's position enhances the receiving sensitivity.

3. Connect a standard UTP cable to the wireless network Access Point. Then, connect the other end of the Ethernet cable to a switch or hub. The wireless network Access Point will then be connected to your wireless network.

4. Connect the AC power adapter to the wireless network Access Point's power socket. Only use the power adapter supplied with the Wireless Network Access Point. Use of a different adapter may result in product damage.

5. Connect the appropriate end of the USB cable to the wireless network Access Point's configuration port. Connect the other end to the USB port on your PC. If your USB port is working properly, your system should immediately recognize the Access Point and attempt to install drivers for it. Continue to the next section for instructions on how to install the drivers.

Now, you are ready to install the drivers for your Access Point. In most computer operating systems, the process happens at least semi-automatically. Generally speaking, the newer the operating system, the more automatic the process is. Here is how to install your Access Point drivers on computers running the Windows Millennium OS:

1. Insert the setup disk into your CD-ROM drive and click "Next" on the "Found New Hardware Wizard" screen.

2. Windows Millennium will automatically identify the wireless network Access Point once it is connected to the PC via the USB cable, and prompt you to install the necessary driver.

3. Select "Automatic Search" for a better driver (recommended) and click "Next." This will search for the Windows Millennium driver.

4. Windows will now install the driver files. Click "Finish" when completed. Your drivers are now installed.

You are now ready to configure your wireless network Access Point. To do this, perform the following easy steps:

1. Insert the setup disk into your CD-ROM Drive. The setup utility should run automatically and an installation screen should appear. If it does not, click "Start" and choose "Run." In the box that appears, enter D:\setup.exe (where "D" is the letter of your CD-ROM drive).

2. When the installation screen appears, click "Install" to start the setup.

3. When the "Welcome" screen appears, click "Next" to continue.

4. A License Agreement screen appears. If you agree with all the terms, click "Yes."

5. The "Choose Destination Location" screen will show you the default destination chosen by the utility. It is recommended that you leave the default destination, but if you want to install this in another location, click the Browse button and select an alternate destination. When you are ready to continue, click "Next."

6. The configuration utility has now been installed. Select "Yes" to restart your PC and then click "Finish."

BUYING YOUR ROUTER

Most wireless Access Points include router capability. This functionality lets you connect your wireless LAN to a cable or Digital Subscriber Line (DSL) modem using a Category 5 cable with RJ-45 connectors. These devices often include a firewall that helps protect your wireless LAN from outside intrusions.

Some of the more popular models, and their prices when this book was published, include the Linksys BEFW11S4 ($129.99) (see Figure 7-5), the Netgear MR314 ($99.99), and the SMC Barricade Broadband Rooter ($149).

CONNECTING YOUR ROUTER TO YOUR NETWORK

If you are interested in connecting your wireless network to your cable or DSL Internet connection, you will need to physically hook up the device, and then configure it to work with your network.

Figure 7-5. The Linksys BEFW11S4 Access Point router.

To hook up your router to your wireless network, perform the following steps:

1. Contact your Web hosting service or Internet service provider (ISP) and ask them for the following information:

   • Your broadband-configured PC's fixed Internet provider (IP) address, if applicable;

   • Your broadband-configured PC's computer name and workgroup name;

   • Your Subnet Mask; and

   • Your default gateway; and your primary DNS IP address.

2. Power everything down, including your PCs, your cable or DSL modem, and the router.

3. Connect a network cable from one of your PC's Ethernet ports to one of the LAN ports on the back of the router (see Figure 7-6). Do the same with all the PCs you wish to connect to the router. (LAN Port 4 will become inactive if you use the Uplink port.)

Figure 7-6. This Access Point router has four ports for Ethernet cable connections.

4. Connect the network cable from your cable or DSL modem to the WAN port on the rear of the router.

5. Connect the power supply cable to the power port on the rear of the router, then plug the supplied AC power cable into a power outlet. The power LED will turn green as soon as the power adapter is connected. The Diag LED (a diagnostic testing mechanism for Light Emitting Diodes used to power displays in electronic gear) will turn red for a few seconds while the router goes through its internal diagnostic test. The LED will turn off when the self-test is complete.

6. Power on the cable or DSL modem. Verify that the power is on by checking the link LED in the WAN column on the front of the Router.

7. The link LED will be illuminated if the power is on and the modem is ready.

Next, you need to configure your PCs to work through your Access Point, and then to your DSL or cable connection. On Windows Millennium PCs, this procedure involves the following steps:

1. Click "Start," select "Settings," then "Control Panel."

2. Double-click the network icon.

3. In the configuration window, select the TCP/IP protocol line associated with your network card/adapter.

4. Click "Properties," then choose the IP Address tab. Select "Obtain an IP address automatically." Click on "Gateway" and make sure that all fields there are empty. Click "OK."

5. The Network Properties window will reappear. Click "OK." All client settings are complete. Windows may ask for original Windows installation files. You should be able to find these on your hard drive (c:\windows\options\cabs.)

6. Windows will ask you to restart the PC. Click "Yes."

7. Repeat steps 1–6 for each PC on your network.

CONFIGURING YOUR ROUTER

It is now time to configure your router to be able to work through your Access Point to access the Internet. To do this, perform the following steps:

1. Open your Web browser and type *http://192.168.1.1* in the browser's address box. This number is the default IP address of your router. Press "Enter."

2. A username and password prompt will appear. Leave the user name box empty and type "admin" (the default password) in the password box. Click "OK."

3. The Wireless AP + Cable/DSL Router's Setup page will appear. The page will ask you to configure a set of "values." These values will be critical to the performance of your wireless network. At this point, it is a good idea to get a basic understanding of what these values mean.

   • Host Name and Domain Name: These fields allow you to supply a host and domain name for the router. Some ISPs require these names as identification. You may have to check with your ISP to see if your Broadband Internet service has been configured with a host and domain name. In most cases, leaving these fields blank will work.

   • LAN IP Address: These values refer to your internal network settings. Unless you have specific internal needs, there should be no reason to change these values. For the internal LAN, the default values are: private IP address, 192.168.1.1; Subnet Mask, 255.255.255.0.

   • Wireless: In this section, you can decide whether or not to use wired equivalent privacy (WEP) encryption and configure the level of WEP encryption. WEP encryption is not necessary for the operation of your router.

   • WAN IP Address: These values refer to the outside network

you connect to every time you access your Broadband Internet connection. Most broadband ISPs assign their clients with a different IP address each time they log on. If this is the case with your ISP, click "Obtain an IP Address Automatically" and go on to the next step. If your ISP assigns you a fixed IP address, click "Specify an IP Address" and enter the address into the Subnet Mask, Default Gateway Address and DNS fields provided by the ISP.

- Point-to-Point Protocol over Ethernet (PPPoE): Some DSL-based ISPs use PPPoE to establish communications with an end user. If you are using a DSL line, check with your ISP to see if they use PPPoE. If they do use PPPoE, you must enable it. If you do enable PPPoE, remember to remove any existing PPPoE applications already on any of your PCs. To enable PPPoE: click "Enable" in the PPPoE section of the setup screen. Enter the user name you use to log on to your Internet connection. Enter your corresponding password.

- Connect on Demand (only available if PPPoE is enabled): If you are not actively using the Internet, you can configure your router to cut your connection with your ISP after a certain period of time. If you have been disconnected because of inactivity, Connect on Demand enables your router to automatically re-establish your connection as soon as you attempt to access the Internet again. If you wish to activate Connect on Demand, choose the Enable option.

- Max Idle Time (only available if PPPoE is enabled): Max Idle Time is the number of minutes that passes before the router drops your Internet connection because of inactivity. For best connection reliability, the recommended settings are 0 or 9999. Otherwise, enter in the number of minutes you want to elapse before your Internet access disconnects.

- Keep Alive Option (only available if PPPoE is enabled): This option keeps your PPPoE-enabled Internet access connected indefinitely, even when it sits idle. It keeps the connection alive by sending out a few data packets periodically, so your Internet service thinks that the connection is still active. To use this option, click "Keep Alive" to select it.

When you have properly configured the setup page, click "Apply," then click "Continue." You are now ready to finish configuring your router. To do so, perform the following steps:

1. On the setup screen, select the DHCP tab. DHCP stands for dynamic host configuration protocol, which automates computer configurations for Internet access.

2. Unless you already have a DHCP server on your internal network, choose "Enable" from the DHCP server field. By choosing Enable, you will configure the router to automatically assign IP addresses to each of your PCs. In the "Number of DHCP Users" box, enter the number of PCs you plan on networking to the router. Do not forget to change this number if, in the future, you add more PCs to your network. In most cases, these values will not have to be changed unless you have more than 50 computers on the network.

3. Click "Apply," then click "Continue."

4. Reset the power on the cable or DSL modem, then restart the computer so the computer can obtain the new router information. Your router is now configured to work with your Access Point.

WHAT YOU HAVE LEARNED

I admit that this chapter is fairly long on technospeak. I wrote this chapter that way because I wanted to give you a good understanding of the very essential building blocks you will need to purchase. These include Network Interface Cards, PCMCIA (Personal Computer Memory Card International Association) cards, Universal Serial Bus equipment, Access Points and routers.

I included basic vendor information and price point for most of this equipment. Of equal importance, I reviewed some essential configuration and installation steps you will need to follow to enable this equipment to run, and to interface with other components that will comprise your wireless network.

WHAT'S AHEAD

In the next chapter, we discuss whether you should build your own wireless network, whether you should contract the whole job out, or use a mixed approach of doing the basic work yourself and then going to experts for the fine-tuning.

TO BUILD OR TO CONTRACT?

Whether we are talking about a wireless personal area network (PAN), a wireless local area network (LAN), or a wireless wide area network (WAN), there are advantages as well as disadvantages to building the network yourself rather than outsourcing the task to a contractor.

BUILDING YOUR OWN WIRELESS PAN

Obviously, if you build your own wireless PAN you will need to handle most of the details yourself. You will need to purchase your own Bluetooth-enabled equipment or upgrade the equipment you already have. This implies some research on your part, to ensure that the desktop computer, printer, scanner, personal digital assistant (PDA), and other components of your network are Bluetooth-compatible. If these components are not Bluetooth-compliant, you may need to replace non-Bluetooth equipment, or add antennas and radio cards to your existing communications and computing devices.

After you acquire new Bluetooth-enabled devices or upgrade your existing devices, you will need to download and install the software on your PC that will enable your wireless PAN to function. In the previous chapter, I explained the software and devices you will need to do this, and while these tasks are not difficult, they may not be your strong suit.

CONTRACTING OUT YOUR WIRELESS PAN

If you choose to contract out your wireless PAN, you will find that such tasks are pretty much "all in a day's work" for consultants and even computer repair technicians. However, not all of these specialists make house calls. A fair portion of this trade views the most lucrative parts of their business as either "workbench" duty fixing computers and computer parts that have been left off at the shop, or doing work in offices. I have long felt that too many shops are a bit behind the times, and do not realize that home offices are real offices, too.

Fortunately, the growing millions of North Americans with home offices have awakened the more perceptive members of the computing service community to the opportunities. Many in this community have leapt at the chance to help, and a fair number of them are fully competent to assist you in setting up your Bluetooth-enabled wireless PAN (see Figure 8-1).

Of course, this option will be somewhat more costly than if you do the network set-up by yourself. Most likely, you will be charged an hourly rate. Although this varies by region, a $65 to $75 hourly rate for wireless network set-up is relatively common. The set-up should not take more than two to three hours. You should be aware, however, that your technician will probably also bill you for the "drive time" it took to get from their last appointment to your office or home. The total for this service comes to approximately $200. That figure assumes a "call out of the blue" scenario, as opposed to additional work in an existing business relationship governed by a service contract.

The $200 fee I just mentioned does not include the cost of the equipment. If your technician works for or has a business relationship with a computer or telecommunications retailer or wholesaler, they may be able to acquire this equipment for you ahead of time. Although the relative newness of Bluetooth supplies has not yet created a substantial market for used equipment, your technician may have access

Figure 8-1. Guardian Computer Support is one of many services that will help you configure your Bluetooth wireless PAN.

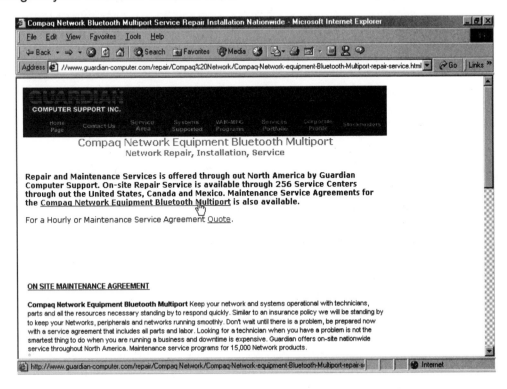

to wireless system components at a slightly lower price than you would pay retail. They may have preferential arrangements with suppliers that will enable them to cut costs to you.

In addition to saving you time and aggravation, your wireless PAN contractor can help in what I call the "peace of mind" department. Having set up your system, he or she will already be familiar enough with it to diagnose problems and implement solutions.

MAKING YOUR DECISION

To contract out your wireless PAN or build it yourself? Clearly the decision is one of cost savings versus expertise. While it is largely the purpose of this book to supply you with the knowledge you need to build your own wireless network, there is no shame in finding the process intimidating. If you have a home office and have a full plate of family responsibilities, you may feel that you just do not have the time to undertake the task yourself.

While I can assure you that building your own Bluetooth-enabled wireless PAN is easier and quicker than you might think, I cannot fault you if you have an irresistible urge to spend that extra $200, and call for help.

BUILDING YOUR OWN WIRELESS LAN

Should you decide to build your own LAN, you will be responsible for equipment acquisition and set-up. Although I have touched on these steps previously, a review of what would fall on your shoulders is appropriate in this context.

In addition to a computer and an Internet connection, you will need to buy an Access Point (see Figure 8-2). Look for equipment that says it supports Institute of Electrical and Electronics Engineers (IEEE) 802.11b or Wi-Fi. Keep in mind that equipment with the Wi-Fi designation has been certified by the Wireless Ethernet Compatibility Alliance as meeting specific wireless network compatibility standards.

Figure 8-2. If you build your own wireless LAN, you will need to purchase your own Access Point. 3Com's AirConnect Wireless LAN Access Point is one of the most popular product lines.

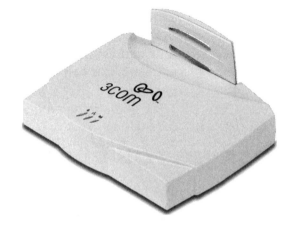

Figure 8-3. Access Points are key components of a wireless network.

You will also need to purchase an access device (see Figure 8-3). Ideally, you should buy your access device from the same company you buy your Access Point from. For a notebook computer, you will need to buy a PC card. These cost $85 and up. For a desktop computer, you should purchase a wireless universal serial bus (USB) client adapter; prices start at about $90.

Set-up comes next. If you are on the fence about whether or not to build your own wireless LAN, it will be helpful to review the steps. These measures follow each other in a logical sequence and are easy to do. To help you decide whether you are up to this task, I feel it would be helpful to go over the steps that you will need to perform to actually enable your wireless LAN.

To install your own wireless LAN on your PC, you will need to perform the following steps:

1. Go to the control panel by clicking "Start," then "My Computer."

2. Write down your current network settings. You may need them to configure your wireless network or restore your network settings if something goes wrong. Note your user name and password, Internet provider (IP) address (if you have a fixed IP address), and your connection method, such as dial-up, cable modem, etc.

3. For laptops, insert the PC card. For desktops, attach the USB client adapter.

4. Insert the CD-ROM that came with your equipment and install the appropriate drivers. Go to the manufacturer's Web site and download any software updates. If you do not have a broadband modem, skip the following two steps.

5. If you have a broadband modem, turn it off. Then, disconnect the Ethernet cable from the computer.

6. Plug in the base station. Attach the Ethernet cable to the port marked "Broadband" or "WAN" and turn your broadband modem back on.

7. Look for a wireless connection utility in the Windows Taskbar in the lower-right corner of the screen. Open it and make sure your PC is getting a signal from the base station.

8. Once you have established a wireless connection, check the instructions for how to configure the base station. If it uses a special software utility, launch it. Otherwise, configure the base station using a Web browser, in which case you'll look for the IP address in the instructions and type that into your browser.

9. Choose a network name, called the service set identifier (SSID), and change the default password (particularly important because hackers are familiar with the factory settings). If you forget your password, you can always reset and reconfigure your base station.

10. Walk around your office and test your wireless network by trying to access it with a laptop or a desktop PC at another location. If you get a connection, congratulations—you've done it!

CONTRACTING OUT YOUR WIRELESS LAN

As with the wireless PAN contracting scenario I described earlier in this chapter, the main tradeoff you will make will be cost versus expertise.

While computer service specialists are available to assist you in setting up your wireless LAN, you will have more service providers to choose from. If you are already getting broadband Internet access from your cable television company, consider contacting them and asking if they offer wireless LAN setup.

Although prices vary, a one-time fee of $350 is relatively common. This includes the Access Point, access device, and the associated labor costs for having a technician come out and get everything running. When you crunch the numbers this comes approximately to a one-third premium over what setting up your own wireless LAN will cost you.

But that cost matrix is just for starters. In a frequent pricing arrangement, each additional PC added to your new wireless network costs $99 to set up. You may also be required to pay a $10 per month maintenance fee for at least one year. That often covers any problems you have on a network of up to four computers.

MAKING YOUR DECISION

Once again, it is a matter of saving on costs versus the "warm and fuzzy feeling" of professional set-up and service expertise. As with wireless PANs, building your own wireless LAN is not difficult. Similar to flying, however, it is not for everybody. But, the fact that you were interested enough to buy this book indicates that you have at least some willingness to undertake the task yourself. From one computer user to another, I say, what the heck—give it a shot.

BUILDING YOUR OWN WIRELESS WAN

In Chapter 4, I discussed how wireless WANs work, and stressed the concept that basically they are groups of interconnected wireless LANs. I listed the tools you will need for bridging these LANs, the security concerns involved in such networks, and I discussed the need to be sensitive to topographical features and buildings that might interfere with system performance.

Building your own wireless WAN is not especially difficult but it does involve a degree of time, commitment, and organizational setup significantly more extensive than for a wireless LAN (and certainly, for a wireless PAN). You will not only incur costs for equipment and software but for extensive site surveys and testing.

CONTRACTING OUT YOUR WIRELESS WAN

If you contract out your wireless WAN, we are not talking about calling a technician and being up and running in just a few hours. Outsourcing to a firm that specializes in wireless network setup and maintenance is far more common. Here, we are referring not to a service call but to an undertaking of project-like proportions.

When government entities, educational institutions, and companies need to find a wireless WAN contractor, they frequently put the project out to bid. The bidding process usually involves a Request for Proposal or RFP.

Not long ago, Eastland County, Texas, put out just that kind of RFP (see Figure 8-4). They attached relative degrees of percentage to various selection criteria. Here are some excerpts from the RFP:

Selection will be based on the following criteria, listed in order of importance:

1. Ability to satisfy program objectives (40 points).

   - Satisfactory response to terms and conditions

   - Satisfactory response to specifications

   - Experience with similar programs

   - Professional reputation, well equipped, well organized, well staffed

   - Customer references and satisfaction of existing customers

2. Cost factors (40 points).

   - Fixed costs

Figure 8-4. An example of a wireless network RFP, as issued by Eastland County, Texas.

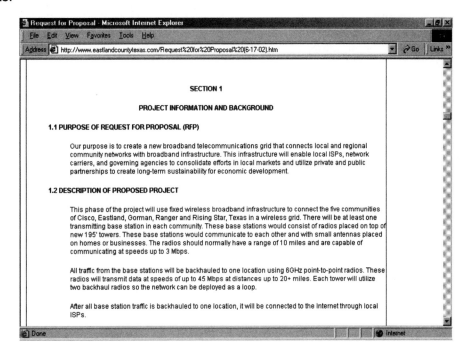

- Reimbursable costs
- Total costs

3. Financial stability (20 points).

- Current financial condition

Obviously, Eastland County placed importance on the ability of the selected contractor to stay in business during the construction time period, and presumably, beyond. If you go that route, you should also ascribe a similar degree of importance. Getting professional references and even a Dun & Bradstreet report is perfectly reasonable.

Eastland County included some other stipulations in their wireless WAN RFP. These included:

- Operations manual: The contractor will provide an operations manual that describes the scope of the network fully, including operation of equipment.

- Project equipment: The contractor will be responsible for safety and operations of all equipment required on the construction site.

- Facilities: The contractor will maintain the site facilities in a clean and safe manner. All trash will be removed from site or stored in a collection container for disposal. The site will be secured at all times when workers are not present.

- Transportation, board, and lodging: The contractor will provide adequate transportation and lodging for all of the contractor's personnel involved in the project. In addition, the contractor will provide sufficient transportation and storage for all of the contractor's equipment.

- Progress reports: As an additional stipulation, Eastland County required the contractor to supply weekly reports during the length of the project timeline, as well as a final report and financial breakdown upon completion.

MAKING YOUR DECISION

Building your own wireless WAN is certainly possible. Given the complexities, the logistics and time factors ramp up significantly over other types of wireless networking projects. The benefits of a wireless WAN are substantial, but the level of commitment to get the technology up and running may or may not be appropriate for your in-house expertise. Hopefully, the information in Chapter 4, as well as the details I have provided you in this chapter, will equip you to make the best decision for your business.

WHAT YOU HAVE LEARNED

In earlier chapters, you learned about the components and equipment necessary to make a wireless network run. Your interest has been piqued and you are ready to give serious consideration to implementing the technology in your business or home office.

As with almost any project, your next decision may well be whether to handle it yourself, to contract it out, or decide on a middle course between these two approaches.

In this chapter, you became familiar with the cost factors involved in each approach. I covered the basic tasks ahead of you if you go your own way, including the all-important planning and benchmarking phases.

Should you wish to go to outside contractors for help, I reviewed general and specific criteria you might use if you decide to look for a contractor. You have learned what they may be expected to do, and how to work with them to structure their project in a practical and efficient timetable that manages your investment of time and effort wisely.

MOVING ON

After you have priced out a wireless networking project, you may need to get approval from your business owner, your Information technology department, or your colleagues. They will want to know all manner of details. Are you already on board but wish that your "superiors" showed the same degree of enthusiasm? The next chapter gives you information and tips about how to get them on board with you.

CHAPTER 9

BUILDING A BUSINESS CASE FOR A WIRELESS AREA NETWORK

In terms of justifying a wireless local area network (LAN), there are tangible as well as intangible factors you should consider. These include return on investment (ROI), as well as operational efficiencies made possible by wireless LAN technology.

The Wireless LAN Alliance (WLANA), an industry trade group, frequently issues studies that seek to quantify the business and operational benefits of using this technology. "Wireless Local Area Networking: ROI/Cost-Benefit Study" is one of the most frequently cited of these surveys.

The Wireless LAN Alliance noted:

Companies that integrate or upgrade with these systems will stretch IT resources further and be able to reap economic and business benefits sooner than companies taking a wait-and-see approach—especially now that a solid standard exists for wireless local area networking . . . As a result of this standard and higher performing or higher speed systems, tomorrow's enterprises will likely have a mix of wireless and wired LAN systems.

To obtain perspective on this issue, the Alliance conducted interviews with information technology managers in several segments, including education, health care, manufacturing, retail, and financial. The survey found that a "successful implementation" occurred in 89 percent of such efforts, and that, on average, full ROI was realized in less than one year.

REAL-TIME INFORMATION ACCESS

One of the consistent findings of the WLANA study was how end-users benefited from real-time information. The association reported that 97 percent of respondents said they either "strongly agree" or "agree" that the wireless LAN contributed to the speed in which they completed a task requiring real-time or near real-time access to information.

COST EFFICIENCIES ARE IMPROVED

"Costs for applications, outsourcing and network management are critical factors that need to be considered before the wireless LAN can either supplement the wired LAN or replace it as a wired LAN alternative," WLANA noted. In terms of money invested, wireless LAN implementation ranged from $300,000 to $4.2 million among survey participants.

The average cost broken down by item, the average percentage of relative costs were as follows:

- WLANA hardware/end-user devices: 50 percent

- Monthly expenses: 1 percent

- Management expenses: 16 percent

- Application development expenses: 16 percent

- Outsourcing: 16 percent

- Downtime: 1 percent

Even with these factors in play, "These savings are substantial from the viewpoint of manufacturer, retailers, hospitals, schools, and financial organizations. A wireless LAN enables them to provide better quality goods, at reduced costs, in significantly less time," the WLANA noted.

Buoyed by these reduced costs, the 12-month payback in ROI kicked in because of increased productivity, organizational efficiency, and the resulting extra gain in revenue and profit.

WIRELESS LAN EFFICIENCIES BY ORGANIZATION

In their survey, WLANA cited implementation advantages specific to the operational characteristics of specific sectors. Here is what the report found, as taken from the report and broken down by sector:

Education

With wireless LANs in place, respondents cited a more efficient use of space and more in-class productivity. At most education sites, the access point was located directly in the wiring closet or in a laboratory. With a wireless LAN, only the access point needs a wired network connection. Classroom or laboratory computers were connected to the access point via radiofrequency (see Figure 9-1).

K–12 schools needed a way to save money on network and computer costs. The Education Rate (E-rate) with 10 percent to 90 percent savings was available, but they needed even more ways in addition to this in order to save. With wireless LANs they were able to save money by buying fewer computers. One key solution involved using cart-mounted computers connected to a wireless LAN. The cart-mounted computers could be moved to the classroom where they were needed. In addition to buying fewer computers, schools also saved money by wiring to a central hub.

Wireless LANs turned out to be very inexpensive on a per-student basis. Wireless infrastructure costs for the educational sector averaged $2,308. In this study 1,345 students benefited from the wireless solution, which in an average configuration included 25 access points and

Figure 9-1. This student is using her notebook computer to communicate over a wireless LAN.

112 computers equipped with wireless adapters. The savings can be attributed to the utilization of cart-mounted computers and fewer network drops as a result of the wireless LAN. With carts, fewer rooms would have needed to be networked and equipped with computers.

Also, because many of the schools had a mandate to get students on the Internet to access more or better learning activities and because the wireless system served as a tool to make this happen, a very fast and easy installation was required. Wireless LANs met their needs in this regard as well. In this study students in the university setting demanded access to LAN resources from dormitories, classrooms, and throughout campus. Wireless LANs were used to help students be more mobile and to help schools reduce network costs and connect remote locations to central buildings and servers. For example, in the university setting, providing a wired connection could be extremely expensive especially if it involved historical buildings. At one site, running wire through ceilings and walls in buildings could have disturbed asbestos insulation, the removal of which was estimated to cost more than $90,000.

Health Care

Because of rapidly rising health care costs, reimbursement and ROI are key to the requirements of Information Technology (IT) investments in the medical industry. Health care costs are increasing at a rate of approximately 5 percent per year, so cost containment is an important issue. Hospitals are centralizing laboratories, reducing costs, and increasing their use of automated technology. Wireless LANS have been shown to meet the technology and organizational demands of health care companies by speeding diagnostic and case analysis turnaround, thus decreasing the length of hospital stays by patients; reducing procedural costs by streamlining procedures, scheduling, and documentation-related tasks (see Figure 9-2).

Manufacturing/Warehousing

Warehouse workers are increasingly demanding mobile scanners or pen-based computing tablets for inputting and accessing data in real-

Figure 9-2. Using a wireless-enabled notebook PC to access information in a medical database.

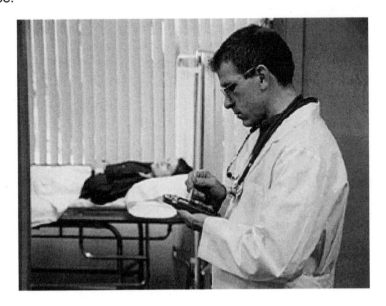

Figure 9-3. The WSS 1040 Wearable Scanning System from Symbol Technologies ties in to a wireless network.

time. These devices are linked to mainframes or servers that usually have a software application such as inventory collection, order fulfillment, and shipping/receiving applications running on them. By connecting to inventory records and purchase orders, companies reduce the inefficiencies of transferring numbers through paper forms. Wireless LANs connected to automated handheld computers on manufacturing or factory floors are a viable alternative to wired LANs. Laying cable in these environments proved to be cost prohibitive or impractical because of the size of the warehouse. Also, changes in assembly lines are frequent and many employees do not work in any fixed location for a given period of time. In this study, we found that workers and management in the manufacturing environment need instantaneous access to accurate information so they can better track orders, production runs, and production quantities in real time (see Figure 9-3).

Manufacturing/Production

Wireless LANs automated the production, maintenance, and troubleshooting (repair) process at production bays of a foundry, production lines of an automotive manufacturer, and the outside work area of an aircraft manufacturer. The use of production planning and control software combined with wireless LAN technology illustrates the positive effect of this specific IT on an organization. A typical medium- to large-sized manufacturing firm must stock, control, and ensure the availability of thousands of items (end products, parts, and raw material). Furthermore, production of the parts and raw material must be coordinated to ensure that the firm meets order commitments and production plans. Using manufacturing software with automated inventory status reporting, order processing, production scheduling, and invoicing features made it possible for companies to control complexity. In this study, however, we found that having a wireless LAN connected to this software enabled operators to go beyond second-guessing the age of the information coming over the wire. It appeared in real-time or near real-time. This combination of hardware and software reduced the control and coordination and associated costs.

Retail

The retail industry category in this study comprised diverse businesses such as restaurants, specialty stores, prepared food stores, and military stores. These stores vary in the types of items they sell and the market size for the items but they all sought faster rates in getting customers through checkout and totaling orders, and faster receipt of goods and taking inventory.

Wireless point-of-sale (POS) cash registers and bar code client devices provide access to store inventory and pricing information. Scanning had a high impact on productivity at checkout because of easier price changing, price removal, and price identification. Price changes can be recorded in a central database at the store rather than on each item.

The wireless LAN infrastructure provided critical decision-makers in retail with real-time information on the ordering, collection, distribution, and sale of goods. The wireless network offered them a higher initial purchase price, but reduced support costs and increased checkout productivity and flexibility (see Figure 9-4).

Financial

The financial/office automation category in the WLANA study comprised a collection of businesses including banking, stock trading, and the consulting, auditing, and office areas of a technology firm; office

Figure 9-4. Retailers use Portable Data Terminals
to transfer information over a wireless network
from warehouses and sales floors into inventory
databases.

automation was a goal for the latter. All of these firms face considerable competition. Keeping up with the competition as well as offering
new services is paramount. In almost every instance the cost-conscious
system manager chose not to standardize exclusively on this new technology because doing so required a large investment in changing the
nearby network infrastructure. Many system managers were attracted
to the wireless LAN for its flexibility, easy installation and, in the case
of the stock exchange participant, mobility.

In the case of banking, the wireless LAN enabled account representatives and tellers to provide better service to customers and has been
used to support a plethora of new transaction processing services. The
auditing and stock trading organizations were just as—if not more—
data-intensive environments, characterized by volumes of accounting,
analysis, and statistical data. The auditing firm was concerned about the
quality of business generated by auditors, as measured, for example, by
the level of engagements handled by the company. But all of these companies need to be able to predict risks and risk factors and facilitating
group collaboration is critical for reaching that goal. In the financial
area, the wireless LAN saved hundreds of hours because group collaboration was easier. Individuals within these organizations are increasingly turning to portable computers to communicate with the home office or master server for various functions. The auditor connected to the
home office through a portable wireless LAN can serve a customer

much more effectively than by dial-up lines, as can sales people and consultants working or collaborating in a conference room.

BEYOND THE NUMBERS: REAL-LIFE TESTIMONIALS

A study commissioned by Microsoft of likely and current wireless LAN users produced a series of compelling arguments for wireless LAN implementation. In going over this list, you may want to note which of these apply to your situation. Also, armed with the ROI and industry implementation advantages cited earlier in this chapter, you will be well on your way to assembling enough information for a preliminary presentation to the decision-makers at your company or institution. After all, these are the people who will need to sign the checks and purchase orders authorizing the building of a wireless LAN. Here are some true-life WLAN advantages, as noted in the Microsoft survey:

- Wireless LAN solves the problem of installing wired network connections in physically inaccessible locations within an office.

- If your company is in an older building that would need to be substantially upgraded for wired network connectivity, the technical limitations of your building are of far less concern for a wireless LAN. Also, it will usually be less expensive to buy wireless units than to have the building rewired.

- Because no wires need to be installed, a wireless network generally can be up and running quicker than a wired network.

- The built-in mobility of a wireless LAN allows information to be input wirelessly without mobile workers having to log on to a new workstation depending on where they are in a building.

- Information entered into wireless-equipped notebook computers and personal digital assistants (PDAs) can be wirelessly transferred into a company database. This reduces the need for these data to be entered when the employee reaches his or her desk. As a result, they can be free to perform other more productive tasks—such as making sales calls.

- Conferencing is easier, especially because wireless-enabled laptops can be brought into a conference room, and then tap into the company's database if needed.

- Wired-network cabling is very difficult to install in some manufacturing and warehouse settings. This is because of the physical parameters and resulting limitations of the factory or warehouse. With a wireless LAN, these concerns are substantially reduced.

- Companies with workers who use notebook computers while they travel do not have to find a phone line in order to log in and access their network.

- With hotels raising phone-related surcharges to unprecedented levels, wireless Internet access via a Wireless Internet Service Provider avoids connect fees, and saves the notebook computer-equipped worker significant money.

- One respondent commented: "If the employees are out of the office, they can still interact with peers and with applications without having to go back to the office."

If you present this information to your company decision-makers, you may get the green light for the planning phase of your wireless LAN. Or you may well be asked for specific information about what cost and logistical factors such an endeavor will entail. These issues are covered in the next chapter.

WHAT YOU HAVE LEARNED

If you are considering a wireless network for your company, you may not have the final say. You may have to cost out, and justify the cost and quantify the ROI (return on investment) to your senior executives, your managers, or your business partners. It may well be that you now have both a commitment and an understanding of this technology that these people have yet to attain.

This chapter gave you some real-world numbers and examples for you to state your case to the decision-makers at your company who may well hold the purse strings.

CHAPTER 10

THE CONSTRUCTION PHASE

In this chapter, we discuss the factors you need to consider as you plan your wireless local area network (LAN), as well as the construction process involved in bringing your wireless LAN to life.

You should start by assessing the suitability of your building and grounds to house a wireless LAN. That process should be followed by a thorough assessment of your current office location or locations.

In evaluating your building and grounds, you should look for, and then consider, the following factors:

- The physical materials of which your building is made.

- Existing devices in the immediate area that could cause interference. These devices could be a heavy electrical power grid, or a cellular phone tower.

- The presence of heavily leafed-trees or heavily sloped grounds, which can block the transmission of line-of-sight radio waves.

- Frequent and severe weather events, such as snow, rain or fog. Bad weather can cause reception problems in and around the network—especially if your wireless network is connected to the outside.

- Your building or buildings' suitability to directional antennas. These structures will be critical to you if you are building a wireless wide area network WAN.

Because of the potential for interference, you should conduct a site survey. If you are renting office space, your facility manager may be able to help. Ask if he or she has any site-survey tools at their disposal. These tools can be used to evaluate the activity already taking place in the part of the radio spectrum in which your wireless LAN components will function. Most wireless equipment vendors bundle these site-survey tools in with their products.

Additionally, you or your facilities manager may wish to use a spectrum analyzer. These devices measure the amplitude of signals on various frequencies.

TESTING INSIDE YOUR BUILDING

You may be moving into an entirely new structure. If your wireless system project includes wired network components such as Ethernet for cabling once the radio signals from your wireless network reach your wired network, you should also test for how well your wired network will run. Although this book does not go into great detail on wired networks, it stands to reason that your planned wireless network will not work well with your wired network if your wired network is prone to performance issues.

Here are some steps you should take to evaluate the suitability of your new building or office for a wired network:

1. Ensure that within the walls, there are pathways that can carry cables throughout your facility.

2. Check the ceilings to determine whether there is enough room to run the cabling.

3. Locate and assess all vertical cabling conduits.

4. Evaluate your electrical system. Confirm that there is enough on-premise power for new components. Pay special attention to the rooms where you will install your network hubs and system servers.

5. Because the servers that wired networks use are especially vulnerable to heat, make sure that your server room is air conditioned, and the cooling equipment is working properly.

6. If your building has been occupied before, research whether your structure has a history of power outages. If this has been the case, you may need to work with your building manager, engineers, and local electrical utility to pinpoint and fix the underlying problem.

IDENTIFYING THE LOCATION OF ACCESS POINTS

In your wireless network, your Access Point will be the central place where your wireless "traffic" will be directed to and from. That is why it is critical for you to place your Access Point in the most optimum location or locations.

The Access Point placement issue becomes especially critical when planning a wireless network for installations with large floors. Examples include warehouses, factories, and hospitals. In some cases, the floor area exceeds the 300-foot limitations of most wireless LANs. For this reason, you will need to be especially cognizant to provide an interface to your wired network, as well as adequate access for your roaming users. Examples include inventory control workers roaming your factory floor, or nurses making their rounds.

Excellent throughput between your devices and your Access Point is usually achievable in completely open areas, which may be completely unrealistic in your facility. After all, the chances are good that your facility has a fair number of obstacles such as walls, desks, and window blinds. Additionally, certain structural and flooring materials can cause obstacles. Plywood is friendly to radio waves; concrete can present some difficulties, and metal structures can cause your wireless communications to degrade significantly.

These structures and objects may impede radio waves from the wireless devices, if not block them entirely. When such unpredictability is introduced, it is difficult to forecast the maximum operating range among all devices. As a result, the optimum location of the Access Point becomes a guessing game.

STRUCTURES THAT MAY BLOCK WIRELESS SIGNALS

These barriers can include:

- Wood: low office partitions

- Plaster: low inner walls

- Synthetic material

- Low office partitions

- Asbestos: low ceilings

- Glass: low windows

- Water: medium damp wood

- Aquariums, which can often be found in executive suites

- Bricked inner and outer walls

- Marbled inner walls

- Paper: high paper rolls

- Concrete: high floors and outer walls

- Bullet-proof glass

- High security booths

- Very high metal desks

- Office partitions

- Elevator shafts made of reinforced concrete

PERFORMING A SITE SURVEY

The most effective way to assess the suitability of placing a wireless LAN Access Point in specific locations is to perform a site survey. You do not need to hire engineers or telecommunications experts to perform this work. Site surveys are easy enough a task for you to do.

Here is what you will need to do your own site survey:

- Obtain blueprints of the facility. If your building is new, contact your architect or developer for a blueprint. If your building is older, you may need to research what changes have been made to the original building. Walls could have been knocked down or new ones put in place. Ceilings and floors may have been re-done with different materials less friendly to wireless signals. Your landlord will probably have this information.

- Do a walk-through. If you do not have access to enough information about changes that may have been made to your floor layout or building structure since initial construction, take the original blueprint and conduct a walk-through of your facility to ensure that nothing major has changed since it was first built.

- You should obtain at least one Access Point from an Access Point vendor. Many vendors will let you test Access Points before you purchase them (see Figure 10-1).

- You will need an appliance that will be used by the users of the system, such as a notebook computer that would be deployed within a wireless network.

- Use a site-survey tool that displays link quality. These software tools are frequently provided by Access Point vendors, and are loaded on to devices (such as network computers) that will communicate with the Access Point. The signal quality and

Figure 10-1. Some Access Point vendors let you try out their products before you buy them.

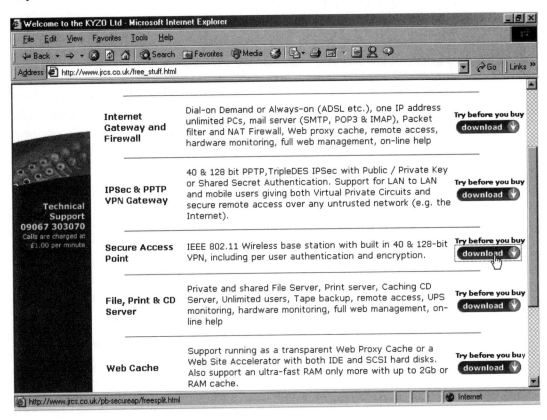

strength is usually indicated by a number. The number scale used varies by Access Point manufacturer.

THAT ALL-IMPORTANT WALK-THROUGH

With your blueprint in hand, you will want to walk through your facility to make sure your blueprint is accurate. This sounds like an easy, "hmm, looks OK" exercise, but it is anything but. When you walk through your facility, you should perform the following steps:

1. Mark permanent user locations, perhaps even using a piece of tape on the floor next to desks where network access will be attempted.

2. On the blueprints, mark the locations of users who will be operating from a fixed location.

3. Mark potential user roaming areas, again, with tape.

4. In addition to the permanent user locations, you should outline potential user roaming areas within the building. In some cases, the roaming areas may be the entire facility.

5. Identify potential obstacles to the radio waves being used. A list of problematic obstacles is included earlier in this chapter.

6. Identify potential sources of interference from the outside. Wireless LAN transmissions can sometimes be interrupted by cellular phone towers and satellite dishes.

7. As you do your walk-through, identify locations where you might wish to place Access Points. Mark these locations on your blueprint.

TESTING YOUR ACCESS POINT

You are now ready to test your Access Point. Install an Access Point and then perform a signal strength test. Ideally, you will want to use a notebook computer. Make sure it has a wireless LAN adapter, and is loaded with the appropriate site survey software (see Figure 10-2).

If you are able to achieve satisfactory performance when you attempt to communicate with your Access Point, you are ready to begin installing your wireless LAN.

Figure 10-2. The Dell Wireless Network Diagnostics Utility is a useful tool for testing the signal strength of a wireless LAN.

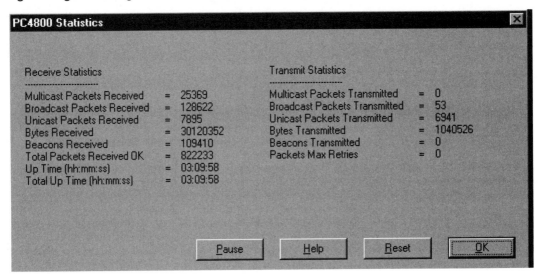

INSTALLING YOUR WIRELESS LAN

Ideally, you will have completed your site survey by now and have identified the optimal conditions and placement for your wireless LAN. Here are the steps you should follow:

1. Develop an installation plan.

2. Coordinate the installation.

3. Stage the components.

4. Install the components.

5. Test the completed installation.

The testing phase is covered in the next chapter. Here are some details for the construction phase, from developing a plan for the installation to the actual installation process.

DEVELOPING AN INSTALLATION PLAN

Before taking components out of the boxes, installing network interface cards (NICs), and setting up antennas, you should spend some time planning the installation. The installation plan is not only a technical schematic, but has a lot to do with project-oriented people management. Here are some steps to take:

- Designate a person to be central contact. Ideally, this should be someone who works in the facility where the installation will take place. They should be able to answer questions related to frequency use and network configuration. This person or persons should also have keys that will let installers into locked rooms.

- Be aware of safety. This is true if you are installing your own network, using staff to do so, or are retaining outside help for at least part of the project. Matters deemed as trivial can affect safety. For example, a metal necklace can dangle into a live electrical circuit and spark an electric shock. Rings can also conduct electricity. If you or your installers are using saws and drills, wear ear and eye protection.

- Select your tools. As we have already discussed, you will want to have test equipment ready. You will need a two-way radio so that your installation team can communicate with each other. Depending on the physical characteristics of your installation, you will also want to keep ladders, flashlights, and crimping tools handy.

- Create a schedule for when the work needs to be performed. Ideally, the least amount of disruption would be evenings and weekends.

- Keep your design documentation handy, so that you or your installers can refer to it right when they need to. If they have to hunt this information down, an episode of "phone tag" or "pager tag" over a weekend can delay matters. If the blueprint is locked in a drawer, and the installers are working on a Saturday, you may not be happy receiving a frantic message while you are at your son's soccer game.

• Create a realistic budget that anticipates costs, and the inevitable "Murphy's Law."

COORDINATING THE WIRELESS LAN INSTALLATION

Once again, this sounds like a simple matter. Communication is key. You should keep facility managers in the loop about the scheduling and—once underway—the progress of the project.

You also need to keep your employees in the loop. If several office areas need to be cordoned off for wireless LAN construction starting this Friday afternoon, give them as much advance notice as feasible. The worst thing you can do is to just have the installers show up near a cubicle, when the occupant is hard at work. With enough advance notice, that employee could be moved temporarily to another desk, or may even choose to work at home during the time the construction phase will impact his or her immediate area.

STAGING THE WIRELESS LAN COMPONENTS

"Staging" is a fairly eloquent term. All it means is that the components necessary for construction are available and handy. Meeting this objective will substantially reduce confusion during the construction process. More importantly, it will help to get your wireless LAN up and running quicker.

To stage your components most efficiently, you should ensure that bulk components are in place. In a wireless network, the bulk components will be boxes of Access Points and radio cards for notebook computers.

Next, you will need to unpack and sort the components. Ideally, you should mark them with the name of each installation site. If you have a radio card for a notebook computer used in a particular department, mark the radio card with that information. You should do the same for Access Points: i.e., "Fourth Floor, Sales Dept., behind carrel 12."

You will then want to ensure the Access Point testing software is routed to the specific devices on your network, and installed on them as well. Do not only "send" the software to your various departments and offices, but follow-up that the software has been installed.

Be prepared to answer any testing-software, installation "how-to" questions. You do not want to begin your actual test, only to find out that some devices that will access the network have the testing software installed improperly or not at all.

INSTALLING THE NETWORK COMPONENTS

It is now time for your components to be installed on your wireless LAN. Consider this procedure analogous to working on the foundation of a new building. Here are the steps you should take:

- Install NICs in the computers that will access your wireless LAN (see Figure 10-3).

- Make sure that you have the correct NIC driver software installed on these machines (see Figure 10-4).

Figure 10-3. The 3Com Gigabit Desktop NIC is a popular Network Interface Card for desktop computers that will interface with wireless networks.

Figure 10-4. Downloading the driver software for the Harmony 7430 OpenAir PC Card.

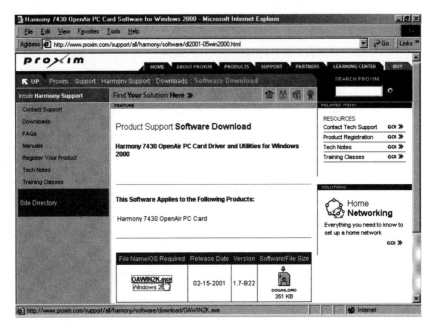

- Install cabling from Ethernet repeaters/switches to the Access Point installation locations.

- Install Access Points with applicable and strong mounting brackets.

- Assemble your server hardware.

- Install and configure your network operating system.

- Install the appropriate software on the user appliances.

Next, you will install your Access Points. Most Access Points have several interfaces, such as RS-485 and RS-232, for connecting a console (terminal or PC running terminal emulation software) to the Access Point for configuration purposes (see Figure 10-5). Some Access

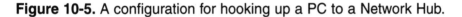

Figure 10-5. A configuration for hooking up a PC to a Network Hub.

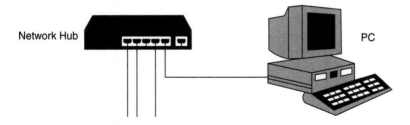

Points even enable you to change configuration parameters via a Web browser or Telnet session if wired network connectivity exists between the Access Point and the PC running the Web browser software or Telnet software. Choose passwords to enable secured access to your Access Points by authorized users.

Even though you have already conducted a site survey to determine where you should place your Access Point(s), a bit of fine-tuning certainly will not hurt. You should mount the Access Points as high as possible. This will increase the transmission range of the Access Point. Do not, however, place the Access Point in a very hard-to-reach location.

Your Access Point came with instructions on how to configure it with the applicable Internet provider and protocol settings. Perform this operation.

Once you complete these steps, it will be a good idea to create a "Network Topology" map. This will be a preliminary map that indicates the physical layout of the network, where everything is located, and the characteristic of the rooms or facilities the wireless network will cover. You should also incorporate a data flow diagram that will list the changes you make to your wireless network. Even small changes, such as the location where a particular employee is likely to access the network, should be indicated.

Do not rule out adding to your data flow diagram during the testing phase. Indeed, you are now ready to test your network. We will discuss this important stage in the next chapter.

WHAT YOU HAVE LEARNED

Implementing a wireless network is far from a matter of buying the right equipment, hooking it up, and putting it to work. Regardless of whether you build your network, or assign the task to staffers or contractors, there are many tasks that must be handled adroitly in the planning and construction phase.

As you have learned in this chapter, these tasks include testing your building for adaptability and potential hindrances to wireless networking transmissions; identifying the best locations in your building or office to place critical network components. Next, you must evaluate the various technical specs and related information you have gleaned during the testing phase, assemble the components, and carefully work out all the specifics you will need to ensure that the upcoming, final testing and installation phases go as smoothly as possible.

CHAPTER 11

THE TESTING PHASE

Just as some of us say "partly sunny," others say "partly cloudy." For some, the glass is "half-empty," for others, "half-full." When it comes to testing wireless networks, a similar philosophical difference can appear.

Some say the reason we need to test these networks is to push them to the limit, determine the outer edge of functionality. We then use these tests to see what might have gone wrong, and fix the problem to achieve even greater performance. Others maintain that we should test networks for ease of use, and whether every person and technical device attached to the network functions intuitively.

In truth, both ways of testing are quite similar to each other. The most efficient testing has reliable and quantifiable results, can be performed with specific equipment, and is rigorous enough to uncover any specific defects that will need to be addressed before your network "goes live."

In this chapter, we cover some of the basics of testing your wireless network before you activate the technology.

TESTING YOUR WIRELESS PAN

You may be setting up a wireless personal area network (PAN) in your home or small office. If so, your test may simply be a matter of seeing if your Bluetooth-enabled devices communicate with each other. Try executing the print command from your notebook or desktop, and see if your Bluetooth-enabled printer "recognizes" it. Perform this function from your computer to your scanner.

Similarly, try to send a screen or a file from your Bluetooth Pocket PC device to that same printer. If everything works, you and your new wireless PAN have passed the test.

USING "AIR SNIFFERS"

For more technically advanced home users, as well as in business environments, however, the testing process should be far more extensive. For this task, you will need a software product called an "air sniffer."

A number of air sniffer software products are on the market. Typically, air sniffer software is controlled by a series of windows and screens that let you configure a test for specific devices, and then perform the actual test.

A number of air sniffers are available. A typical starting price is around $1,000. Because many are similar, I selected the FTS For Bluetooth Air Sniffer from Frontline Test Equipment, Inc., to illustrate the air sniffer testing process.

To perform an air sniffer test of your wireless PAN using FTS for Bluetooth, perform the following steps:

1. Connect the BTComProbe to an available universal serial bus (USB) port on your PC.

2. Open the FTSBLUE folder on your PC desktop and double-click on the Air Sniffer Icon. The Data Source Control Window will appear (see Figure 11-1).

3. Open the Set I/O Parameters Window by clicking on the Set I/O Parameters Button on the Data Source Control Window.

Figure 11-1. The FTS For Bluetooth Air Sniffer Data Source Control Window.

4. Select the piconet synchronization mode, the method by which FTS for Bluetooth synchronizes with the piconet, from among the three synchronization techniques: Slave Inquiry, Master Inquiry, and Passive Slave Page. For the purposes of this test, choose Slave Inquiry (see Figure 11-2).

5. Specify the synchronization device by selecting the targeted device from the drop-down list.

6. You now need to prepare to capture data from the test to a memory buffer on your computer, or to a floppy disk. To do this, you will need to access the Data Control Source Window, and then, the Control Window. To do so, click the Resync Button. Next, click the Start Sniffing button.

7. To capture data to a buffer click the Start Capture to Buffer button. To capture data to a file, click the Start Capture to File button. FTS for Bluetooth will ask you to name the file.

8. To end the sniffing, click the Stop Sniffing button.

ANALYZING YOUR SNIFFING SESSION

At this point, you will have your choice of several ways to analyze your just-concluded "sniffing session." Some of these methods involve deciphering detailed information that can resemble code or equations. In the interest of simplicity, let us stay away from these.

Figure 11-2. Selecting the Slave Inquiry option enables FTS For Bluetooth to synchronize with a piconet.

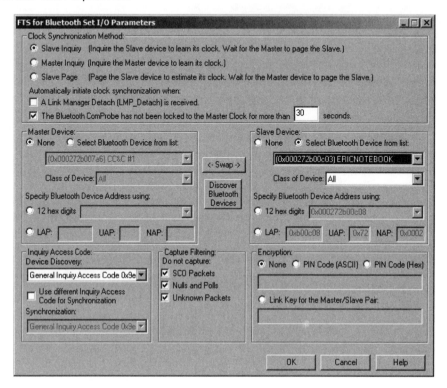

Instead, we will cite the functions of FTS For Bluetooth's Statistics Display screen (see Figure 11-3).

On this screen, you will be able to analyze system performance for the entire sniffing session, and the number of errors caught by the sniffer. You will reach the Statistics Display window by clicking the percentage icon in the top toolbar of the FTS For Bluetooth main graphical interface (see Figure 11-4).

TESTING YOUR WIRELESS LAN AND WAN

To test your wireless network, you will need link test software. This software should have come bundled in with your Access Point hard-

Figure 11-3. The FTS For Bluetooth Statistics Display screen is set up to show the results of a test session.

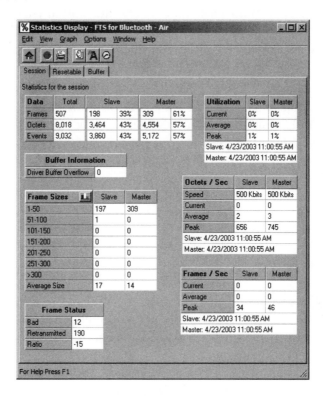

Figure 11-4. To reach the FTS For Bluetooth Statistics Display window, click the percentage icon on the main FTS For Bluetooth window.

ware. Once you install your link test software, it will work with your Access Points, and the devices they attach. A test will determine the quality of transmissions between the station (radio card in the appliance) and the access point.

During the test, special packets of information will be sent out through the network. The testing software will see that another packet is sent back to the sending station. Based on the sequence numbers of the packets being sent back and forth, the station running the link test will be able to tell you whether the link is corrupting data packets on the forward or return leg of the link.

Here are some of the factors that link test software looks for:

- The percentage of frames successfully sent within a given test.

- Average, maximum, and minimum times it takes the Access Point to receive a response from the destination.

- Average, maximum, and minimum strength of the signal at both ends of the link.

- Average, maximum, and minimum amount of retries the network attempts when packets are sent or received unsuccessfully.

The test works by continuously polling the station's carrier sensing functions and displaying the percent of time the station (such as a notebook computer) senses a busy medium. Most link test software allows you to adjust the parameters for different performance levels. Among network engineers, the general consensus is that you should set the test to transmit at the highest bit rate possible, and to send at least several hundred test transmissions. That testing framework conforms to the "worst case scenario" I intimated at the beginning of this chapter.

HOW THE TEST WILL WORK

The outcome of performing test cases is test results. A perfect result does not necessarily mean that the test was "too easy." At the same time, however, poor results will probably indicate a need for you to re-work your network design. Just as likely, you may need to reconfigure your components, such as your Access Point. Perhaps you have too many devices on the wireless network, or your wireless network is picking up interference from outside sources.

Fortunately, your testing software will be able to identify the problem or problems. It will do so by offering baseline measurements you will be able to compare with established quality standards.

UNDERSTANDING THE TESTS YOU SHOULD PERFORM

Before you go live with your wireless network, a successful test should include the following four procedures:

1. Unit testing.

2. Integration testing.

3. System testing.

4. Acceptance testing.

DOING UNIT TESTING

Unit testing will check the configuration and performance components on your wireless network. These components can be network interface cards, Access Points, servers, cables, or even printers. You will want to unit test each component before trying to make them work with other parts of the system. This way, you will know that one or more pieces of this equipment are not defective. If you are able to rule this in (or out) before you start the integration testing phase, you will save time by not having to backtrack.

No need to worry with high-end details here. That is because most components have built-in self-tests that run whenever you turn the device on, or they have test utilities that you can run manually; therefore,

Figure 11-5. Category 5 cabling attaches wireless networks to wired networks.

you usually will not need to develop specialized test cases for a unit.
You may already know that when you turn your printer on, it will attempt self-diagnosis by printing a test page. A notebook or desktop
computer will go through a corresponding exercise, and will note any
problems before it is able to complete a boot-up. Similarly, some wireless LAN products, for example, come with a utility that verifies
whether you have specified information or settings that conflicts with
other hardware on the network.

You will also want to test the Category 6 or, more likely, the older
Category 5 cable that attaches your wireless network to your wired
network (see Figure 11-5). When something is wrong, your two networks will not be able to communicate with each other. Most often,
the problem is physical rather than settings-oriented in nature. In this
context, physical could mean a failing connector, a loosely attached
wall plate, or just simple corrosion of the cable itself.

A cable tester is the main piece of equipment you will need at this
stage. The Fluke Networks OMNIScanner2 (see Figure 11-6) is one of
the most popular. It is not inexpensive, and can cost more than $5,000.
That may sound like a lot of money, but it can help you pinpoint problems that may cost you many multiples of that amount to fix later on.
If the price-point is still a bit of a budget-buster for your business,
some electrical supply wholesalers make this hand-held device available for rental.

The cable tester will perform a series of attenuation tests. The device will look at whether or not your cabling is sending and receiving
signals at relatively consistent frequencies throughout the network. If

Figure 11-6. The Fluke Networks OMNIScanner2 is one product you can use to test your network connections. Photo courtesy of Fluke Networks.

PentaScanner®

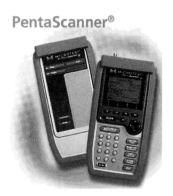

it does not, you may receive transmission errors. These transmission errors will surely result in retries that—if numerous enough—can delay transmissions.

Most attenuation tests work by sending a series of signals at different ranges within the cable's operating frequency bandwidth. A series of tests ranging from 1 megahertz to 100 megahertz in 1-megahertz increments is often recommended. By performing the examination in this manner, the cable tester will be able to pinpoint errors at specific frequencies.

A cable tester also measures a phenomenon known as crosstalk. That means the crossing of current from one wire to a nearby wire. When this unfortunate circumstance occurs, transmission errors often result.

For an accurate measurement, cable testers record crosstalk levels by stepping through the cable's operating frequency range at very small increments, such as 0.25 megahertz all the way from 1 to 100 megahertz. Although we are talking about some 400 steps here, a good cable tester should be able to complete this task in 30 seconds or less.

Most cable testers are able to pinpoint any problems by specifying the frequency at which the problems occurred. Specific diagnosis based on what frequency the problems occurred is beyond the scope of this book. A good cabling or telecommunications engineer will gain a heads-up if they have access to this information.

COMPLETING INTEGRATION TESTING

Integration testing confirms that all the components of a wireless network are working together. Even though the component pieces of the network function swimmingly on their own and the network cards are working well, problems can still exist.

For example, you might not be able to log on to your server from your notebook PC via your Access Point. Perhaps, your network interface card and Access Point were configured to work and communicate on different channels. As you might expect, the result will be, as Strother Martin said to Paul Newman in the film classic, *Cool Hand Luke,* "What we have here is a failure to communicate."

The key point to look for in an integration test with a wireless notebook, for example, is how well the notebook communicates with the network at various places on the network. Take your notebook computer and try to access the network from different cubicles within the range of your wireless local area network.

GEARING UP FOR SYSTEM TESTING

System testing will help you determine whether the completed network installation will be able to meet the requirements you expect for your wireless network. By this stage, you will ideally have installed all the components, and performed the appropriate tests I have just described.

ACCEPTANCE TEST: THE FINAL TESTING PHASE

An acceptance test will check whether all users can access the needed applications from their desktop or notebook computers. It will check the security settings, and make sure that in the case of a wireless WAN, that a seamless interchange between wireless LAN is possible.

This stage is especially critical to wireless LAN-wireless WAN performance. If, for example, you have a wireless WAN that connects hand-held inventory-checking devices deployed at your store with your four warehouses, and you use your wireless network to communicate orders between a hand-held device at a store with the warehouse closest to that store location, a problematic transmission can result in delayed and lost orders—and lost customers.

TROUBLESHOOTING YOUR WIRELESS LAN

Even with a perfectly tested wireless LAN, glitches can result. Here are some common wireless LAN problems, and how to fix them:

- If your Access Point does not power up, make sure your power source is operating. Confirm that all cables are correctly connected to the Access Point.

- If one of your computers cannot connect with your wireless LAN, confirm your device's Network Name. Each wireless PC Card in the Access Point should have a unique Network Name. This Network Name must match the active Network Name on client machines. For example the ORiNOCO Client Manager software allows you to store Network Names in configuration profiles, then you can select a profile to fit your location. If you do not know your network name, check with your network administrator.

- If your connection goes in and out, make sure your devices are within the signal range limits of your network. If they are, and you are still having problems, check the signal strength gauge built in to your Access Point software.

- Should you not be able to connect to the Internet wirelessly through your access point, open the Web-browser interface of your Access Point software. Most of this software has a Configure button and a Network tab; click both. Doing so will ensure that the proper Dynamic Host Configuration Protocol (DHCP) settings are being used. As noted earlier, DHCP is an Internet protocol for automating the configuration of computers that are used to access the Internet.

• Alternatively, you can check to see that your local DHCP server is operating on the same network as your Access Point. From the computer where the Access Point software is running, use the "ping" network command to test the connection with the Access Point. If the Access Point responds, but you still cannot connect to the Internet, there may be a physical network configuration problem. At this point, you may be in a bit over your head. Such situations justify a network support person, whom you should contact next.

If your wireless network has passed the preoperational tests you have put it through, you are just about ready to launch the network into the real world. First, however, you will want to have a system in place to manage what you have just built. I cover wireless networking administrative and security issues in the next chapter.

WHAT YOU HAVE LEARNED

Any wireless network needs to be tested before its formal launch. In this chapter, you learned about the basics of such testing.

For wireless Personal Area Networks, these tests include basic task-driven tests and security-confirming Air Sniffer sessions. This chapter explains how to do both.

For wireless Local Area and Wide Area Networks, you will need to conduct Unit Testing, Integration Testing, System Testing, and Acceptance Testing. True, these tasks sound intimidating, but they can be accomplished quickly and for the most part, by the use of relatively inexpensive equipment.

Some tests may indicate problems. I concluded this chapter with a brief review of some problems that might come up during the testing phase, and how you might be able to fix them.

CHAPTER 12

MANAGING YOUR WIRELESS NETWORK

When it comes to managing technology, a plan that encompasses decisions about operational control is best finalized ahead of actual implementation.

This chapter covers some general points and offers some suggestions about wireless personal area network (PAN) and local area network (LAN) management. We start by discussing some key elements of a wireless networking management plan. Then, we transition to a substantive discussion of security related wireless network management issues for both main types of wireless networks.

TRAINING IS KEY

Training is necessary before your wireless network goes live. Your system administrators, network and telecommunications staff, as well as your users should know how to support and operate your wireless network efficiently.

Once in place, your wireless network will be used by your employees, your management staff, and quite possibly your contractors and customers. The users should be trained on how to run the application software associated with your wireless network. For instance, they should know their way around Access Point software, and be familiar enough with the command structure for reaching the network so that they will not constantly need their hands to be held.

I recommend that you hold on-premise training sessions. You should also work with your information technology (IT) staff and vendors to draft and write a plain-English, illustrated, procedural manual about how to log on to and use your new wireless network.

System administrators and support staff need an enhanced level of training as well. Supervisors—technical and not—ought to have at least a basic understanding of how to diagnose the most common network operating system problems. Your system administrator should be fluent with the configuration of the network (such as Internet provider [IP] address assignments of all Access Points and appliances).

ESTABLISHING A HELP DESK

A centrally located Help Desk will be the first place your end-users turn with their wireless networking related problems. The Help Desk need not be at the same facility as your employees but the Help Desk Staff should be aware of the issues your employees and other end-users may face.

Here are some suggestions to ensure that your Help Desk provides the most benefit to your employees who are using your new wireless network:

- Establish a central phone number for your Help Desk, and post it throughout your facility. Few things are more frustrating than an already stressed employee fighting a technical glitch—

and having to ask around for the Help Desk's telephone number.

- Give your Help Desk personnel live training. If possible, have them participate in final pretesting. Involve them in actual wireless network transmissions. Why? It is important for them to have a "real feel" for this system. Too many Help Desk administrators give their charges a sheet of symptoms and solutions. Not that this is a bad idea, mind you. Yet, the solution for so many telecommunications and computing problems is a series of improvised "work-arounds" that might not be included in a help sheet.

- Establish a knowledge base. Knowledge bases are incident reports and recommended solutions. Often, these resources refer to specific problems that have occurred. Successful solutions to these problems are catalogued, and then grouped in case files. These case files are searchable by keyword.

- Post your knowledge base on your company Intranet. This way, an employee having difficulty with your wireless network will be able to search the knowledge base. There are two possible outcomes, both of them good. He or she may find the answer they need, saving your Help Desk time and effort. Or, your employee may not find a solution but by virtue of having searched the knowledge base, will have given your Help Desk personnel a headstart on ruling out common problems as a cause to whatever the glitch is.

- Keep an adequate number of Help Desk personnel on duty at all times, including evenings and weekends where practical. To determine staffing levels, log the time of each Help Desk inquiry.

- Put your IT and wireless network service people on your Help Desk from time to time. This way, they will get a sense of "real world" issues. Sensitivity to the end-user is not always found at the IT level, but it should be.

MONITORING YOUR NETWORK

Network monitoring seeks to find problems in the network before issues arise. Access Points and radio cards usually maintain a management information base. These bases can store statistics on system performance, and errors. Have a system in place for your network administrator to regularly check the numbers and other data crunched by these information bases.

A STITCH IN TIME: PERFORM PREVENTIVE MAINTENANCE

With any technology, some problems can be fixed more easily when they are detected as minor glitches. Set up a procedure to perform preventive maintenance on the network, and troubleshoot and repair the network if it goes down. Keep spare Access Points, radio cards, and other components around and on the premises if possible. Do not wait for your wireless network to go down entirely. You do not want to be reduced to pleading with your suppliers for an overnight shipment of a critically needed replacement.

LIST YOUR COMPONENTS

As you use your wireless network, you may need to do periodic adjustments and upgrades. There are several things to consider. The ability of newly upgraded or added hardware or software to function smoothly in an integrated environment is key. Smart advance planning for system upgrades involves cataloging the equipment you have, their capabilities, their interfacing eccentricities, and their compatibility issues.

At minimum, you should record the type and model number of your network interface adapters, as well as all your equipment, such as

Access Points and switches. List the phone number and E-Mail address for the key contact and support people at each hardware and software vendor with equipment on your wireless network. Note what operating system you use, the cabling standard for connecting to your wired network, and the vendor-support plans you have enrolled in. Odds are you will need all this information at some point.

When you have compiled all this information, place it on your company Intranet for all authorized users to access.

PLAN FOR DECISION MAKING

You may have hundreds, or even thousands, of users on your wireless network. There needs to be an infrastructure in place to assess periodic upgrades. Establish a technical review panel that can assess prospective changes, and whether the changes are practical and feasible. This panel should not only comprise technical people, but at least one staff member (or consultant) with an understanding of the specific costs involved.

Once the technical review panel signs off on an upgrade, you will then be in a position to present the proposed upgrade to senior management for their approval. You should also simultaneously work with your Help Desk to make plans for training sessions and updated technical manuals.

BENCHMARKING IS KEY

If you have the necessary elements in place for your wireless network upgrade, work with your technical and support staff to determine project timelines and benchmarks. Ensure that you have provided enough time to deal with the inevitable Murphy's Law. No matter how carefully you plan and execute, there may be problems such as late hardware shipments, software with version conflicts, and a training schedule that may cause some interference with daily operations.

PLANNING FOR SECURITY

Even the most technically efficient and well-managed wireless network will be of little use if the network is not secured. Security is not as much a matter of preplanning as it is of ongoing policies, controls, and countermeasures, when necessary.

A public document by the U.S. Department of Commerce's National Institute of Standards and Technology (NIST) offers the following pointers for administering secure wireless LANs:

- Identify who may use wireless LAN technology in an organization.

- Identify whether Internet access is required.

- Describe who can install Access Points and other wireless equipment.

- Provide limitations on the location of and physical security for Access Points.

- Describe the type of information that may be sent over wireless links.

- Describe conditions under which wireless devices are allowed.

- Define standard security settings for Access Points.

- Describe limitations on how the wireless device may be used, such as location.

- Describe the hardware and software configuration of any access device.

- Provide guidelines on reporting losses of wireless devices and security incidents.

- Provide guidelines on the use of encryption and other security software.

- Define the frequency and scope of security assessments.

Another management countermeasure is to ensure that all critical personnel are properly trained on the use of wireless technology. Network administrators need to be fully aware of the security risks that wireless LANs and devices pose. They must work to ensure security policy compliance and to know what steps to take in the event of an attack. Finally, the most important countermeasures are trained and aware users.

IMPLEMENTING SECURITY COUNTERMEASURES

NIST suggests the following security-related policies and technologies for wireless networks.

Physical Security for Access to Wireless Computer Equipment

This security should be designed to minimize the risk for improper penetration of facilities, such as rooms where Access Points are kept. Effective countermeasures can include external boundary protection, and even biometric technologies such as palm scans, hand geometry, iris scans, retina scans, fingerprint, voice pattern, signature dynamics, or facial recognition.

Secure Access Point Placement

NIST counsels that an Access Point not be placed where part of its range extends beyond the physical boundaries of the office building walls. This is because an individual outside the building could eavesdrop on network communications by using a wireless device that picks up the signals being sent through the network. NIST also suggests this course for secure wireless wide area networks (WANs).

Use Technical Countermeasures

Technical countermeasures involve hardware and software solutions to help secure the wireless environment. Software countermeasures include proper Access Point security settings, as well as software patches and upgrades, authentication, intrusion detection systems (IDS), and encryption. Hardware solutions include smart cards and biometrics.

Secure Your Access Point by Updating Default Passwords

This sounds obvious, but there are excellent technical arguments for updating the default passwords. Most wireless LAN devices come with their own default settings, some of which inherently contain security vulnerabilities. Notes NIST:

> The administrator password is a prime example. On some Access Points, the factory default configuration does not require a password (i.e., the password field is blank). Unauthorized users can easily gain access to the device if there is no password protection. Administrators should change default settings to reflect the organization's security policy, which should include the requirement for strong (i.e., an alphanumeric and special character string at least eight characters in length) administrative passwords.

Establish Proper Encryption Settings

Encryption settings should be set for the strongest encryption available in the product, depending on the security requirements of the organization. Typically, Access Points have only a few encryption settings available: none, 40-bit shared key, and 128-bit shared key. The strongest is 128-bit.

Control Your Reset Function

This function also sounds basic, but it can cause real havoc if not managed well. That is because the reset function automatically purges a new security setting the network administrator has applied to the Access Point. NIST points out:

> The default settings generally do not require an administrative password, for example, and may disable encryption. . . . An individual can reset the configuration to the default settings simply by inserting a pointed object such as a pen into the reset hole and pressing. If a malicious user gains physical access to the device, that individual can exploit the reset feature and cancel out any security settings on the device. The reset function, if configured to erase basic operational information such as IP address or keys, can further result in a network Denial of Service, because Access Points may not operate without these settings. Having physical access controls in place to prevent unauthorized users from resetting Access Points can mitigate the threats. Organizations can detect threats by performing regular security audits.

Be Alert to Software Patches and Upgrades

Many software vendors (not just wireless networking software vendors) offer periodic security patches and upgrades. Some of these vendors announce these upgrades via E-Mail alerts, and provide these patches for download on their Web sites. You or your network administrator should visit the Web sites of all your software vendors and look to see if a patch-alert E-Mail service is available. If such is provided, sign up. You will not regret doing so. An additional list of security vulnerabilities and patches is maintained on the NIST site at *http://icat.nist.gov* (see Figure 12-1).

Consider an IDS

An IDS is an effective software tool for determining whether unauthorized users are attempting to access, have already accessed, or have compromised the network. A network-based IDS will be able to monitor the network traffic on a LAN or a LAN segment, packet by packet,

Figure 12-1. An additional list of wireless security vulnerabilities and patches is maintained on the NIST site.

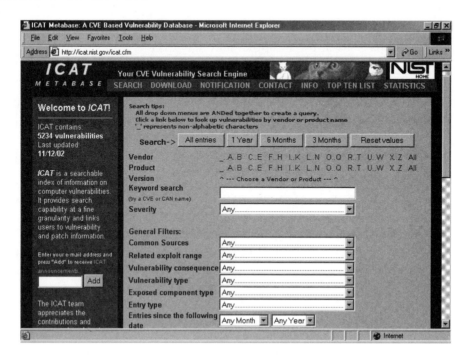

in real time (or as near to real time as possible) to determine whether traffic conforms to activities that match known attack patterns. If the IDS detects such untoward activity, the network monitor built into the product (see Figure 12-2) will recognize packets that conform to this pattern and take action such as killing the network session, sending an E-Mail alert to the administrator, or other action you may prespecify.

Perform Periodic Security Audits

Use network analyzers such as NetStumbler (*www.netstumbler.com*) to see if wireless products are transmitting on the correct channels. If not,

Figure 12-2. Network monitor utilities built into Intrusion Detection systems can point out unauthorized attempts to access a wireless network.

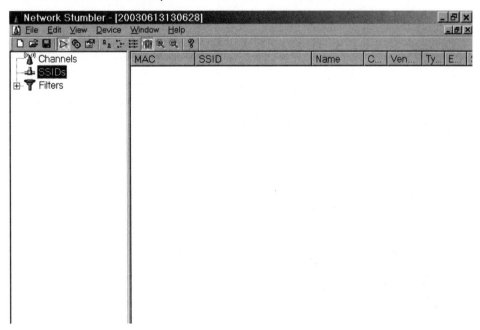

it is at least possible that someone "on the inside" is tampering with your system. This software is downloadable from the NetStumbler site. It works on most wireless networking cards.

Consider Smart Cards

Smart Cards are tamper-resistant devices that are inserted into equipment terminals on wireless (or wired) networks. User information, such as biometric data, is stored on smart cards. If an end-user works on more than one machine, these cards can provide the extra benefit of portability, as well as network security.

The U.S. Department of Commerce's National Institute of Standards and Technology offers these tips for administering a secure wireless LAN:

Security Recommendation	Checklist		
	Best Practice	May Consider	Done ?
Develop an organizational security policy that addresses the use of wireless technology, including IEEE 802.11.	✓		
Ensure users on the network are fully trained in computer security awareness and the risks associated with wireless technology.	✓		
Perform a risk assessment to understand the value of the assets in the organization that need protection.	✓		
Ensure that the client Network Interface Card (NIC) and Access Point (AP) support firmware upgrade so that security patches may be deployed as they become available (prior to purchase).	✓		
Perform comprehensive security assessments at regular intervals (including validating that rogue APs do not exist in the IEEE 802.11 Wireless LAN) to fully understand the wireless network security posture.	✓		
Ensure external boundary protection is in place around the perimeter of the building or buildings of the organization.	✓		
Deploy physical access controls to the building and other secure areas (e.g., photo ID, card badge readers).	✓		
Complete a site survey to measure and establish the AP coverage for the organization.	✓		
Take a complete inventory of all APs and IEEE 802.11 wireless devices.	✓		
Empirically test AP range boundaries to determine the precise extent of the wireless coverage.	✓		
Ensure AP channels are at least five channels different from any other nearby wireless networks to prevent interference.	✓		
Locate APs on the interior of buildings versus near exterior walls and windows.	✓		
Place APs in secured areas to prevent unauthorized physical access and user manipulation.	✓		

Security Recommendation	Checklist		
	Best	May	Done
Make sure that APs are turned off all hours they are not used.	✓		
Make sure the reset function on APs is being used only when needed and is only invoked by an authorized group of people.	✓		
Restore the APs to the latest security settings when the reset functions are used.	✓		
Change the default service set identifier (SSID) in the APs.	✓		
Disable the "broadcast SSID" feature so that the client SSID must match that of the AP.	✓		
Validate that the SSID character string does not reflect the organization's name (division, department, street, etc.) or products.	✓		
Disable the broadcast beacon of the APs.		✓	
Understand and make sure all default parameters are changed.	✓		
Disable all insecure and nonessential management protocols on the APs.	✓		
Enable all security features of the Wireless LAN product, including the cryptographic authentication and WEP privacy feature.	✓		
Ensure that encryption key sizes are at least 128-bits or as large as possible.	✓		
Make sure that default shared keys are periodically replaced by more secure unique keys.	✓		
Install a properly configured firewall between the wired infrastructure and the wireless network (AP or hub to APs)	✓		
Install antivirus software on all wireless clients.		✓	
Install personal firewall software on all wireless clients.		✓	
Deploy MAC access control lists.		✓	
Consider installation of Layer 2 switches in lieu of hubs for AP connectivity.		✓	
Deploy IPsec-based Virtual Private Network (VPN) technology for wireless communications.		✓	

Security Recommendation	Checklist		
	Best	May	Done
Ensure encryption being used is as strong as possible given the sensitivity of the data on the network and the processor speeds of the computers.		✓	
Fully test and deploy software patches and upgrades on a regular basis.	✓		
Ensure all APs have strong administrative passwords.	✓		
Ensure all passwords are being changed regularly.	✓		
Deploy user authentication such as biometrics, smart cards, two-factor authentication, or PKI.		✓	
Ensure that the ad hoc mode for IEEE 802.11 has been disabled unless the environment is such that the risk is tolerable.	✓		
Use static IP addressing on the network.		✓	
Disable Dynamic Host Configuration Protocol (DHCP).		✓	
Enable user authentication mechanisms for the management interfaces of the AP.	✓		
Ensure management traffic destined for APs is on a dedicated wired subnet.		✓	
Make sure adequately robust community strings are used for SNMP management traffic on the APs.	✓		
Configure SNMP settings on APs for least privilege (i.e., *read only*). Disable SNMP if it is not used.	✓		
Enhance AP management traffic security by using SNMPv3 or equivalent cryptographically protected protocol.		✓	
Use a local serial port interface for AP configuration to minimize the exposure of sensitive management information.		✓	
Consider other forms of authentication for the wireless network such as RADIUS and Kerberos.		✓	
Deploy intrusion detection sensors on the wireless part of the network to detect suspicious behavior or unauthorized access and activity.		✓	

Security Recommendation	Checklist		
	Best	May	Done
Deploy an 802.11 security product that offers other security features such as enhanced cryptographic protection or user authorization features.		✓	
Fully understand the impacts of deploying any security feature or product prior to deployment.	✓		
Designate an individual to track the progress of 802.11 security products and standards (IETF, IEEE, etc.) and the threats and vulnerabilities with the technology.		✓	
Wait until future releases of 802.11 Wireless LAN technology that incorporates fixes to the security features or enhanced security features.		✓	
Make sure the wireless "network" is fully understood. With piconets forming scatternets with possible connections to 802.11 networks and connections to both wired and wireless wide area networks, an organization must understand the overall connectivity. Note: a device may contain various wireless technologies and interfaces.	✓		
Ensure that the handheld/small Bluetooth devices are protected from theft.	✓		
Make sure that Bluetooth devices are turned off during all hours that they are not used.	✓		
Take a complete inventory of all Bluetooth-enabled wireless . devices.	✓		
Study and understand all planned Bluetooth-enabled devices to understand any security idiosyncrasies or inadequacies.	✓		
Change the default settings of the Bluetooth device to reflect the organization's security policy.	✓		
Set Bluetooth devices to the lowest necessary and sufficient power level so that transmissions remain within the secure perimeter of the organization.	✓		
Make sure the Bluetooth "bonding" environment is secure from eavesdroppers (i.e., the environment has been visually inspected for possible adversaries before the initialization procedures during which key exchanges occur).	✓		

Security Recommendation	Checklist Best	Checklist May	Checklist Done
Choose PIN codes that are sufficiently random and avoid all weak PINs.	✓		
Choose PIN codes that are sufficiently long (maximal length if possible).	✓		
Ensure that no Bluetooth device is defaulting to the zero PIN.	✓		
Configure Bluetooth devices to delete PINs after initialization (to ensure that PIN entry is required every time) and is not stored in memory after power removal.	✓		
Use an alternative protocol for the exchange of PIN codes (e.g., the Diffie-Hellman Key Exchange or Certificate-based key exchange methods at the application layer—Use of such processes simplifies the generation and distribution of longer PIN codes).		✓	
Ensure that combination keys are used instead of unit keys.	✓		
Invoke link encryption for all Bluetooth connections regardless of how needless encryption may seem (i.e., no Security Mode 1).	✓		
Make use of Security Mode 2 in controlled and well-understood environments.	✓		
Ensure device mutual authentication for all accesses.	✓		
Enable encryption for all broadcast transmissions (Encryption mode 3).	✓		
Configure encryption key sizes to the maximum allowable.	✓		
Establish a "minimum key size" for any key negotiation processes.	✓		
Ensure that portable devices with Bluetooth interfaces are configured with a password or PIN to prevent unauthorized access if lost or stolen.	✓		
Use application level (on top of the Bluetooth stack) encryption and authentication for highly sensitive data communication. For example, an IPsec-based Virtual Private Network (VPN) technology can be used for highly sensitive transactions.		✓	
Use smart card technology in the Bluetooth network to provide key management.		✓	
Install antivirus software on intelligent, Bluetooth-enabled hosts.		✓	

Security Recommendation	Checklist		
	Best	May	Done
Fully test and deploy software Bluetooth patches and upgrades on a regular basis.	✓		
Deploy user authentication such as biometrics, smart cards, two-factor authentication, or PKI.		✓	
Deploy intrusion detection sensors on the wireless part of the network to detect suspicious behavior or unauthorized access and activity.		✓	
Fully understand the impacts of deploying any security feature or product prior to deployment.	✓		
Designate an individual to track the progress of Bluetooth security products and standards (Bluetooth SIG) and the threats and vulnerabilities with the technology.		✓	
Wait until future releases of Bluetooth technology incorporates fixes to the security features or offers enhanced security features.		✓	

MANAGING YOUR WIRELESS PAN SECURELY

In most cases, Bluetooth-enabled wireless PANs more or less "manage themselves." This is because their configuration is simpler than wireless LANs, and does not require the organizational complexities of bigger networks. Because the machines on a Bluetooth network function with each other more or less as they would on a wired network, the end-user does not have to learn as many access technology pointers. Still, a basic training session is advisable, as is the drafting of documentation for your new wireless PAN.

All this is not to say there are not some very effective security measures you can implement. Because most hardware-related security solutions for Bluetooth are built into the Bluetooth devices themselves, the accent is on the software.

NIST suggests that in addition to the PIN codes or passwords your end-users work with to access your wireless PAN, that you "[E]mploy device authentication as an extra layer of security. Incorporating application-level software that requires password authentication to secure the device will add an extra layer of security. Organizations with both high- and low-end–users should incorporate application-level software that requires password authentication in Bluetooth devices."

A Personal Digital Assistant (PDA) that requires a password for access, or a specific desktop program that mandates the same, are examples of password authentication.

The U.S. Department of Commerce's National Institute of Standards and Technology offers these tips for administering a secure wireless PAN:

Area of Concern	Security Threat/Vulnerability	Risk Mitigation Solution
Device physical security	At risk from malicious users that "sniff" transmissions in an attempt to intercept data.	Built-in frequency hopping technique prevents some disclosure.
	At risk from malicious jamming and interference from other devices that operate in the same band.	Maintain secure perimeter around devices in network.
		Require devices to operate at lowest power management level so that transmissions remain within the secure perimeter of the organization.
Short PINS are used, PINs are stored in nonvolatile memory, and poor distribution exists.	PINs are guessed or compromised. Automatic connections are established.	Use PINs that are as long as possible (e.g., 16 bytes).
		Ensure that PINs are not stored on Bluetooth devices but are deleted for sensitive applications.
		Develop a PIN distribution scheme or implement smart card approach.

Area of Concern	Security Threat/Vulnerability	Risk Mitigation Solution
Device authentication methods	Man-in-the-middle attacks. Device authentication.	Make sure authentication occurs on all transactions.
		Ensure mutual-authentication is enabled so that both devices in a transaction are verified.
		Do not share the unit key with untrusted sources.
		Implement password security software.
Encryption	Eavesdropping occurs on unprotected links.	Make sure encryption is enabled on all transactions. Do not use Security Mode 1.
		Ensure that the Bluetooth device is configured to use broadcast encryption.
		Ensure that the key size is configured for maximal lengths —ensure that an acceptable "minimal key length" parameter is set.
	The stream cipher may be weak and broken over time. Some encryption algorithms are more robust (e.g., 3DES and AES) than others (e.g., RC4 and DES); weaker algorithms can be easily cracked.	Use highest level of encryption possible for wireless communications. Applications-level encryption using public, well-known, more robust algorithms can be deployed.
Authorization	Bluetooth device connects and gains unauthorized access to applications on another device.	Implement Bluetooth Security Mode 2 with appropriate access policies established.

Area of Concern	Security Threat/Vulnerability	Risk Mitigation Solution
Security patches upgrades	Vulnerability that may yet be discovered can be fixed through patches.	Monitor the release of Bluetooth security patches. Test and update security patches and upgrades in a timely manner to limit the likelihood that older versions of software are being used that may contain security vulnerabilities. Note: none of these are known to exist at this time.
Device Internet/E-mail access	Viruses.	Incorporate and regularly update virus software.
	DoS attacks.	Implement software that monitors management messages that suggest DoS attacks.
	Data are vulnerable to third-party providers.	Use only a trusted third-party provider.
Poor design of built-in Bluetooth security (e.g., bad random number generator)	Adversary exploits a security feature that is not properly designed by the Bluetooth manufacturer. The result is compromised system security (e.g., unauthorized access to a device, unauthorized disclosure of information).	Fully understand the security of Bluetooth products that are deployed. Request manufacturers to provide full disclosure through white papers or provide third-party assessment reports. Do not purchase devices of which the security cannot be determined.
Uncertainties about the built-in security of the algorithms and procedures	Adversaries can defeat some of the mechanisms that are thought to be secure.	Monitor developments surrounding Bluetooth security. Seek guidance from security experts specializing in Bluetooth wireless communications.
Privacy violations	Adversaries can determine the person associated with a Bluetooth device and monitor activities.	Be vigilant about where a Bluetooth device is used. Note: Because of the public parameter address disclosure, not much can be done in this regard.

WHAT YOU HAVE LEARNED

Even the best-planned wireless network will fail without proper management and maintenance.

I wrote this chapter to introduce some best practices that will help you "feed and water" your wireless network once it is up and running. By reading this chapter, you learned about training, customer support, equipment inventory control, and other measures you can take to ensure that your wireless network has the best chance of running seamlessly.

Not all potential "bad news" comes from within the network, however. Your wireless LAN or PAN may be degraded by security issues, including probes, hacks and attacks from the outside. That is why I devoted significant space to specific countermeasures you might take to keep your network secure from prying ears and eyes.

MOVING ON

Technology marches on. Even the best-run wireless network may need upgrading. Deciding when to upgrade, and how to manage the process, is the subject of the next chapter.

CHAPTER 13

UPGRADING YOUR EXISTING WIRELESS NETWORK

If you are already using wireless networking technology, you will want to be alert for upgrades. These upgrades fall into one of two categories: significant enhancements or new editions of specific technical components that comprise your network.

When you do upgrade, you will need to manage the process smoothly. This chapter gives you the basic information you need about upgrades, so that you can decide which of these enhancements your wireless network cannot do without, and then be able to oversee the upgrade.

BASIC WIRELESS TECHNOLOGY UPGRADES

The Institute of Electrical and Electronics Engineers (IEEE) 802.11 is the basic technology used for wireless local area networks (LANs) and wide area networks (WANs). It is constantly being improved upon. These improvements are researched by, and then approved by committees of the IEEE. The technologies that roll out are not necessarily improvements based on letter order. For example, the 802.11a-based products currently on the market are significantly faster than 802.11b-based products. That is because the standards are based on the name of the committee that developed them.

As new standards are developed, each is listed in and is available from the IEEE Web site at *http://standards.ieee.org/wireless/index.html* (see Figure 13-1).

Figure 13-1. The IEEE Web site has the latest news about new and changing wireless network technical standards. © 2003 IEEE

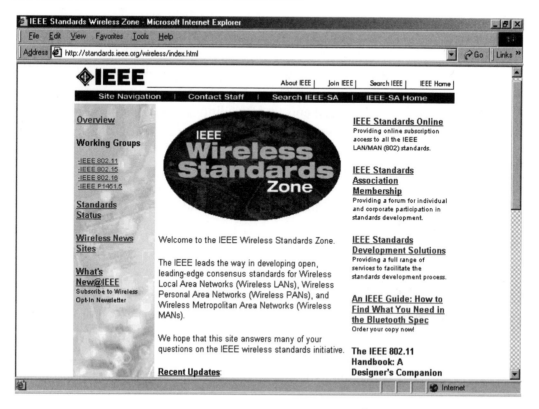

Here are the key wireless technologies now in effect or in development at the time this book was written as described on the IEEE Web site:

- The IEEE 802.11 specifications are wireless standards that specify an "over-the-air" interface between a wireless client and a base station or access point, as well as among wireless clients. These are the standards for wireless LANs.

- The IEEE 802.15 Working Group provides, in the IEEE 802 family, standards for low-complexity and low-power consumption wireless connectivity. These are the standards for Bluetooth-enabled wireless personal area networks (PANs).

- IEEE 802.16 specifications support the development of fixed broadband wireless access systems to enable rapid worldwide deployment of innovative, cost effective, and interoperable multivendor broadband wireless access products. These are the standards for wireless WANs, which the IEEE generally refers to as Metropolitan Area Networks.

A GUIDE TO IEEE 802.11 ALPHABET SOUP

For your purposes, the three main families of 802.11 standards and products you should be aware of are 802.11a, 802.11b, and 802.11g. Individual wireless networking products are certified by IEEE as compatible with one of the three technologies.

I will not get overly technical, but here are some basic things to take into account as you make your decision:

Speed

IEEE 802.11a (also known as Wi-Fi 5) and 802.11g products are faster than 802.11b products. The first two standards provide 54 megabits per second transmission speeds. IEEE 802.11b (Wi-Fi) products have a maximum transmission speed of 11 megabits per second. If your key reason for installing a wireless LAN is to enable your users to have wireless access to the Internet, then any type 802.11 connectivity is your best choice.

Network Capacity

When network capacity is your primary criterion, go for 802.11a, because 802.11a and 802.11g can achieve the same speeds. As a result of the increased number of nonoverlapping channels that 802.11 provides, you will be able to set up more Access Points closer to each other.

Your Office and Building Layout

Research shows that 802.11a-compliant products, while fast, seem to have difficulties transmitting around and through glass. You will be pleased to learn that 802.11g products do not have this problem. That is because these products transmit on a different frequency—one that seems to be considerably more impervious to blockage than those products that use 802.11a.

Backward Compatibility

If your wireless LAN is already up and running with 802.11b-compliant equipment, 802.11g may be the best choice for an upgrade. You will be able to add 802.11g Access Points and stations at your own pace, or as you detect that certain groups of users need faster wireless LAN access.

KEEPING CURRENT WITH STANDARDS

When it comes to 802.11, 802.15, and 802.16 standard improvements, the update information provided by IEEE tends to be overly technical in nature. For wireless LAN-related 802.11 scuttlebutt, it will be far more useful for you to track this information by periodically visiting the 802.11 Planet site at *www.80211-planet.com.* For the latest information, check the Tutorials section of the site (see Figure 13-2).

For Bluetooth-wireless PAN news, check the Bluetooth site at

Figure 13-2. The Tutorials section of the 802.11-Planet site has the latest news about wireless LAN standards and equipment. Reprinted with permission from http://www.80211-planet.com Copyright 2003 Jupitermedia Corporation.

www.bluetooth.com. In time, there will be an 802.16 site for most wireless WAN users. Until then, check the IEEE site *(www.ieee.org)* for the latest news (see Figure 13-3).

KEEPING CURRENT WITH NEW PRODUCTS

Both the 802.11 Planet and the Bluetooth site I just mentioned are great resources for new product information.

At *http://products.80211-planet.com/802.11_products/*, new products are grouped in more than twenty categories. These categories include Access Points, Access Point power supplies, antennas, network

Figure 13-3. Checking for IEEE news about the emerging 802.16 wireless networking standard. © 2003 IEEE

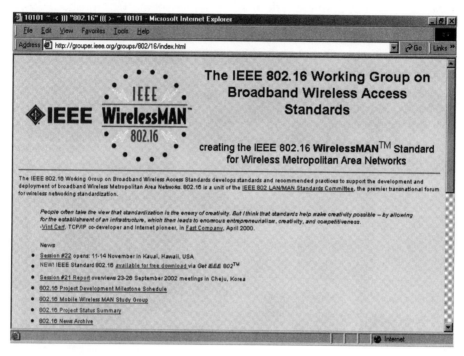

monitoring equipment, plus laptop computers and Personal Digital Assistants (PDAs) preconfigured to work in a wireless LAN (and, in most cases, in a wireless PAN as well). The listings are keyword searchable, and lead to articles that in most cases have links to the manufacturer's Web sites. In turn, most manufacturer sites have detailed product information, case histories, and offer the ability to buy the product online from the site itself (see Figure 13-4).

Similarly, the Qualified Products section of the Bluetooth site lists all Bluetooth-compliant products. At the end of 2002, there were more than eight hundred such products listed. These are divided into groups, such as Bluetooth-compliant printers, etc. Each product is listed by

Figure 13-4. IEEE 802.11-Planet's site maintains a list of wireless LAN-compatible products. Reprinted with permission from http://www.80211-planet.com Copyright 2003 Jupitermedia Corporation.

name, product serial number, and the most recent update date. There is usually a link to the manufacturer's Web site as well (see Figure 13-5). Yet you should be aware that many of the listed products are not end-user devices, but components of primary interest to manufacturers of Bluetooth devices.

For simplicity, that is why I recommend regularly checking the Web sites of the companies that make your Bluetooth-enabled devices. Ever eager for promotion, these manufacturers will frequently tout new and upgraded models of these printers, PDAs, scanners, and so forth (see Figure 13-6).

Figure 13-5. For a list of Bluetooth-compliant products, visit the Qualified Products section of the Bluetooth site. Copyright 2003 bluetooth sig, inc.

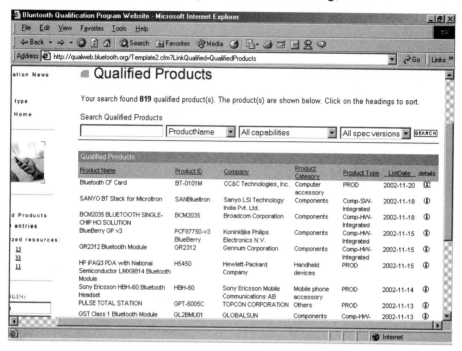

MANAGING YOUR WIRELESS PAN UPGRADE

When new Bluetooth-compliant products are released, they should work automatically with your existing wireless PAN. Whether to buy them or not may simply be a matter of price versus performance. Your decision to upgrade may not be directly related to the Bluetooth-compliant attributes of the product, but to the additional functionalities it offers.

For example, a Bluetooth-enabled PDA with a rich color display might be a significant improvement over a similar device without a back-lit screen. A scanner with a larger screen might offer more functionality than the smaller scanner you are now using. A new printer might print more pages per minute than the currently installed model.

Figure 13-6. Many computing products sites tout the wireless compatibility of new products.

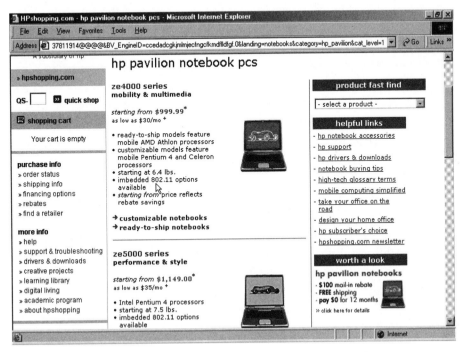

In these cases, you are not upgrading your wireless PAN per se, but upgrading the hardware that comprises the network.

MANAGING YOUR WIRELESS LAN UPGRADE

Plainly, wireless network upgrades have the potential for chaos if not managed effectively. Rather than fall for enthusiastic marketing talk, you should first assess whether the wireless networking product or operating system is really necessary.

I discussed site surveys in the previous chapter. You should have obtained enough data from the site survey to predict which groups of users will use your wireless LAN most frequently. Odds are they will be the ones who will be clamoring loudest for a system or product upgrade. They may ask for an upgrade because the number of transmissions sent out over the network has significantly increased with time but speed has suffered some as a result.

In such cases, the type of product you buy should be dictated by the symptoms called to your attention. For example, if you need to increase your wireless network's capacity, you may need to add new Access Points. Recently, Access Points have become available with two PC card slots. Access points such as the ORiNOCO AP 2000 will give your network nearly twice the capacity of an Access Point with only one such slot (see Figure 13-7).

In other instances, updates are necessary to correct security or operational "bugs" in a specific product. To stay abreast of these opportunities, periodically check the Web sites of your equipment suppliers. Additionally, see if these sites offer automatic E-Mail notifications of new products and fixes. Most of us do not have time to keep checking vendor sites, but we do check our E-Mail.

Finally, here are some general tips to manage your wireless LAN upgrade more efficiently:

- Write down all the settings for each device in the existing network. Your product software may enable you to save this information to a file on your hard drive. If not, print out all the configuration option screens in the software that comes with each product.

Figure 13-7. Newer Access Points, such as the ORiNOCO AP 2000, come with two PC card slots.

- If you are upgrading more than one product, handle each upgrade individually. Test the network after each product upgrade. That way, you will be able to catch glitches as they occur, and then attribute them to the product if you need to. Take it from me—this method will be far less aggravating rather than performing a mass upgrade and then trying to find out what devices on the network are causing the problem.

- Write down, save, or print all the new configuration settings for your product and system upgrades.

- After you have installed all the new products, perform a thorough system test under real conditions. To minimize disruption in your office, conduct the test during an evening, or even over a weekend.

- Once your upgraded system is functioning in real time, conduct a new site survey to determine usage patterns, as well as any unforeseen glitches that may not have come up during the testing process you engaged in immediately before your upgrade.

WHAT YOU HAVE LEARNED

Just as you upgrade your home entertainment center or back deck, you might wish to upgrade your wireless network. Hopefully, the case will be driven by the growth of your business. As I noted at the start of this chapter, these upgrades fall into one of two categories: significant overall enhancements to your network, or upgrades to specific technical components and equipment that make your network run.

There are some easy and quick ways to stay abreast of wireless technology upgrades you might consider and evaluate which of these upgrades are mission-critical, or at least desirable. Once you gather this information, you will want to manage the upgrade process in an orderly way.

I hope that this chapter gave you a workable road map to handling these decisions and procedures efficiently.

MOVING ON

In the next chapter, we cover the exciting new technology of wireless broadband, and how to integrate that functionality into your wireless network.

CHAPTER 14

UNDERSTANDING WIRELESS BROADBAND ACCESS

Hopefully by now you are sold on the advantages of a wireless local area network (LAN). With a wireless LAN, you will be able to tie in several computers and other devices for fast and secure communications, with or without a minimum of wires and cables.

The computers on a LAN may be able to communicate with each other but what about over the Internet? If you already have fast Internet access through one PC, you will be able to extend that capability to all the desktops and notebook computers on your wireless LAN.

Think of the upside. You already may be using your fast Internet connection to send and receive large graphics and PowerPoint files in the wink of an eye. If you build a wireless LAN, you will not have to play favorites as to which of your employees "gets to use" the computer with the quick Internet connection. With as much magnanimity as you please, you will be able to spread that capability throughout your entire network.

EXTENDING BROADBAND OVER A WIRELESS LAN

Making your broadband Internet connection available to all the computers on your wireless LAN is a slightly different process for cable modem and Digital Subscriber Line (DSL) fast Internet access. This section describes the process for cable modem users.

If you are already using a cable modem to access the Internet and want to have that capability throughout your wireless LAN, you will need to follow five basic steps. These are:

1. Hook up your cable modem unit to your Wi-Fi Access Point.

2. Make sure that all your computers are hooked up to your wireless LAN.

3. Install the necessary support software.

4. Test what you have done so far.

5. Add other computers to your installation.

Now, I will detail the procedures for each of those five steps.

ATTACHING YOUR CABLE MODEM TO YOUR Wi-Fi ACCESS POINT

This step will ensure that your Access Point will be able to send and receive signals from your cable modem. As a general rule, you cannot depend on the installer from your cable company to help you. That is because cable companies generally limit their technicians to helping with the initial cable modem installation. For some reason, they view an extension of the cable modem service throughout a wireless LAN as being outside their field of expertise. A cynic may view this policy as attributable to the fact that the cable company would earn no extra revenue from several subscribers sharing one line—so it would not be in their best interest to have an "on the clock" installer provide such a service.

With that in mind, I am afraid you will be on your own. But not to worry—the process of attaching your cable modem to your Access Point is a simple process involving the following steps:

1. Turn off the power to your computer, as well as to your cable modem.

2. Unplug your computer and the Access Point from their electrical outlets.

3. Disconnect the Ethernet cable that connects the cable modem to the Ethernet card in your computer, while leaving the Ethernet card plugged into your cable modem. You will be using the same Ethernet cable that connects your desktop computer to your cable modem.

4. Plug one end of the Ethernet cable into a jack in the Access Point (see Figure 14-1).

5. Plug the other end of the jack into your cable modem.

6. Plug the cable modem and your Access Point back into the electrical outlets.

Figure 14-1. Plugging an Ethernet cable into a wireless network Access Point.

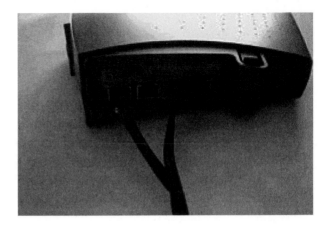

HOOKING YOUR COMPUTERS UP TO YOUR WIRELESS LAN

At this point, you should already have drivers installed on your wireless LAN. Every computer on your network needs to have an installed and configured universal serial bus (USB) unit or a Wi-Fi card. If that is not the case, the individual computer will not even be hooked up to the wireless LAN. You will need to add these PCs to your network by installing the unit or card, and then ensuring the correct driver software is in place to operate the device on the individual PC.

The next section describes how to install the ORiNOCO USB Client on a PC, either one that is intended for a wireless LAN or a stand-alone (see Figure 14-2).

First, you will need to install the client manager software that comes with the USB Client. Then, you will hook up the USB Client itself. To accomplish this procedure, perform the following steps:

Figure 14-2. This ORiNOCO USB client is awaiting the installation process.

1. Remove your ORiNOCO USB client from its box (see Figure 14-2). Place the device near your computer.

2. Insert the ORiNOCO CD-ROM that came with your kit in your CD-ROM drive. Your operating system will automatically start the CD and display a blue Main Menu box.

3. In the Main Menu box, click the Install Software button.

4. In the Main Menu box, click "Install Client Manager." Connect your ORiNOCO USB Client to the USB slot at the back of your computer (see Figure 14-3). You will be prompted to locate the driver installation files.

5. Select the ORiNOCO CD-ROM included with the USB Client Kit and browse to the folder that matches your operating system.

Figure 14-3. Connecting the ORiNOCO USB Client to the USB slot at the back of a wireless network-enabled computer.

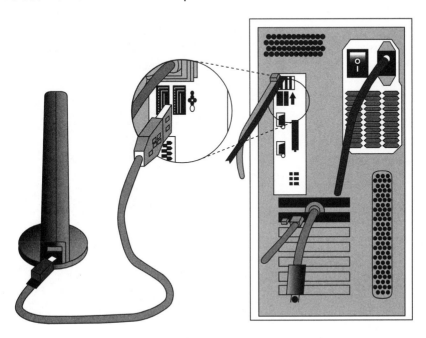

6. Windows should start the "Add New Hardware Wizard" automatically. You are now ready to install the necessary drivers.

7. If this is the first time that network support is installed onto your computer, the Network screen will appear (see Figure 14-4).

8. The Windows operating system will prompt you to enter a computer and workgroup name. These names will be used to identify your computer on the Microsoft Network Neighborhood. In the computer name field, enter a unique name for your computer. In the workgroup field, enter the name of your workgroup.

9. After installing the drivers, Windows will open the Add/Edit Configuration Profile window for your ORiNOCO USB Client. The Add/Edit Configuration Profile window enables you to specify one or more network connection profiles. Select "Office," and then, "Connect to an Enterprise Network via an Access Point."

Figure 14-4. The Network screen helps the user configure the USB Client.

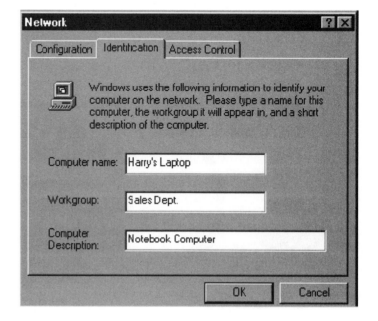

10. In the Network Name field, define the name of the wireless network to which you want to connect. You can use: the value "ANY" (all characters uppercase), to connect to any wireless LAN network in the vicinity of your computer, or an "exact" value to connect to a specific wireless network. Consult your LAN administrator for the value that applies to your network. The Network Name can be any alphanumeric string in the range of "a" to "z," "A" to "Z," and "0" to "9" with a maximum of 32 characters.

11. Click "OK" to confirm and return to the Add/Edit Configuration Profile window.

12. Click "OK" again. You will have completed this installation.

HOOKING UP YOUR NOTEBOOK FOR SHARED BROADBAND ACCESS

You may wish to set up one or more notebook computers for broadband Internet access over your wireless LAN. The process for hooking up and then installing the drivers for a PCMCIA card varies by manufacturer and operating system. This section reviews the procedure for Windows NT, a popular Windows operating system for offices.

To ensure that your notebook computer(s) is set up to accept broadband Internet access over your wireless LAN, perform the following steps on each machine:

1. Turn your notebook computer off.

2. Insert the Ethernet card into a PCMCIA socket (see Figure 14-5).

3. Turn the computer on and let Windows load.

4. Open Control Panel, and then access your Devices menu. Go to the PCMCIA listing and click on it.

5. Double-click "Network."

Figure 14-5. By inserting an Ethernet card into a PCMCIA socket, the user is preparing to hook up his notebook computer for fast broadband Internet access.

6. Click "Adapters."

7. Select "Add." You will see a list of network cards. Select "Have Disk." Insert the installation diskette into drive A:

8. Because you are running Windows NT4, type A:\WINNT40 and then click OK.

9. Select the "PCM-ET-S10x PCMCIA Ethernet Card" and click "OK." The Network Card Setup box appears.

10. Select a free IRQ and free I/O Port. Set the Bus Type to PCM-CIA and Number to 0 then click OK.

11. At this point, you will be ready to configure your network settings and protocols that have come with your Access Point software.

INSTALLING YOUR SUPPORT SOFTWARE

You are now ready to run the software that came with your Access Point. This process was described in Chapter 10. As part of this process, most Access Point software comes with an installation procedure that includes a connection box. Depending on the product, the connection box may have choices for cable modem and DSL. You will highlight the choice that most closely describes your method of broadband Internet connectivity.

TESTING YOUR INTERNET CONNECTION

Because you have now configured your Access Point software to work with your cable modem, you have reached the appropriate point for testing your setup. From a connected computer on your network, enter the address of any Web page. See if the computer you are using is able to access the page. If so, you are connected. You may wish to further test your installation by accessing a page with lots of photographs, or even with audio and video. Such pages contain more "information," and generally take a fairly long time to load over a dial-up Internet connection. If you configured your network properly, that should no longer be a problem. Quite literally, your connected computers will be up to speed!

ADDING COMPUTERS TO YOUR BROADBAND LAN

To add more computers to your broadband LAN, simply repeat the processes for hooking up your desktop or notebook computers as I described earlier in this chapter.

ADDING BROADBAND INTERNET ACCESS TO YOUR WIRELESS WAN

When you tie in a group of wireless LANs via a network bridge, you have formed a wireless wide area network (WAN). If all the computers and Access Points at different locations throughout your wireless WAN are properly equipped as described in this chapter, you should be enabled for broadband access. At the time this book was written, the Institute of Electrical and Electronics Engineers (IEEE) was working on a highly technical standard to boost the performance of devices used in such systems.

HOOKING UP YOUR WIRELESS LAN TO DSL

Many offices and homes access the broadband Internet via DSL—a fast method of Internet access over phone lines—rather than cable.

In all probability, your LAN Access Point is configured with a Dynamic Host Configuration Protocol (DHCP) server. This feature automatically configures all properly equipped computers on your network to be connected to the Internet. If each of your computers has the right card and driver software installed as described above, you will want to choose "DSL" at the appropriate sequence in your Access Point software installation.

WHAT YOU HAVE LEARNED

We live in a broadband world. That is especially true when it comes to Internet (and Intranet) connectivity. Dial-up just is not fast enough!

In Chapter 5, you learned how to connect your wireless network-enabled notebook computer to the Internet—while out on the road.

High-speed Internet connectivity is also possible over devices hooked up to a wireless Local Area Network. This procedure varies some by equipment and network configuration, but is not difficult. Reaching this goal may also involve several procedures, each with definite steps.

These procedures may well include attaching your cable modem to your Wi-Fi Access Point, hooking your notebook computer up to your wireless LAN, equipping your notebooks or other devices for shared broadband access, and even hooking up your wireless LAN to your DSL (Digital Subscriber Line), should that be your existing method of high-speed Internet access.

This chapter walks you through these, as well as additional processes relevant to obtaining wireless broadband access through your wireless network.

MOVING ON

By now, you have gained a basic understanding of how wireless networking works. You know the tools that you will need and the procedures you will follow to build your own wireless PAN, LAN, or WAN. The next—and final—chapter summarizes the key points in this book, and takes a look at the exciting enhancements to wireless networking that are in the offing.

CHAPTER 15

PUTTING IT ALL TOGETHER

Before you read this book, you may not have had an accurate under-standing of wireless networking technology. I would be willing to bet, though, that like me, you often found yourself grappling with a spaghetti-like mixture of cables underneath your computer desk. You have no doubt encountered this in your office, too.

Do not misunderstand me: I love wires. I built a radio when I was an eight-year-old Cub Scout. Here in my cliffside home in Portland, Oregon, just about every wall socket is in use. So when it comes to wires (and everything else, for that matter), I have no prejudices.

Still, there is a far superior way to ensure that computers and the devices that work with them are tied together. While we are talking about Access Points and built-in radios, we are also talking about using air to communicate. As a species, we have been communicating through the air far longer than we have over wires. It is a poetic stretch—but not an inaccurate one—to say that when it comes to how we communicate, wireless networking takes us back to our roots.

With that in mind, let us review what has been covered in this book.

I started out with an overview of wireless networking and why it is likely to be the right technology for your business communication needs, followed by an overview of different types of wireless networks.

In Chapters 2 through 4, we looked at wireless personal area networks (PANs), local area networks (LANs), and wide area networks (WANs). We explored how they work, the equipment that each configuration consists of, and issues related to getting up and running.

In Chapter 5, we explored how you can prepare your notebook computer to work over your internal wireless network, as well as over the Internet.

In Chapter 6, we took the wireless networking technologies explained in the previous chapters, and covered some case histories about their use in real-life situations ranging from a chiropractic clinic to a plant that makes jet engines.

I thought Chapter 7 would be a good place in the book to take you to market and have you shop for wireless networking equipment. Then, I covered the basic installation steps you need to perform once those parts arrive, or you get back to your home or office with them.

Even though the theme of easy-to-build wireless networks runs throughout this book, I realize that at some point you may experience the temptation to hire a contractor. (Nothing against contractors: my contractor brother-in-law has given my sister a wonderful and fulfilling life.) At the least, I felt I owed you an objective pro-and-con examination of retaining a contractor versus building your wireless PAN, LAN, or WAN yourself. It is my hope that the information I presented in Chapter 8 has helped you make that decision.

Regardless of whether you hire a contractor or build your own wireless network, someone has to pay for it. That someone could be you or it could be your company. If the latter is the case, chances are that you will need to present your case to decision-makers who will sign the purchase orders and the checks. In Chapter 9, I took you through the various persuasive arguments at your disposal, as well as presented real-life testimonials from representatives of companies that have implemented wireless networking and that would never go back.

With the assumption that you have now been "sold"—or have sold your superiors—on a wireless network, I covered the planning and construction phase in Chapter 10. As you read that chapter, you learned how to perform the various planning-related testing and site surveys prior to your wireless network installation, as well as how to manage the installation process efficiently. I cannot overstate the importance of an organized planning and construction procedure.

When your wireless network is in place, you should perform a dress rehearsal to ensure that all the equipment and software you set up will work cohesively. Chapter 11 gives you some key pointers for this all-important part of the process.

If you have successfully gone through the testing phase with your new wireless network, you are ready to go live. But even though you have planned and tested diligently, an up-and-running wireless network needs to be maintained diligently. Preventive maintenance must be performed regularly, end-users must be able to find answers to their questions, and most importantly, the network must be made and kept secure from interlopers. I explored these issues in Chapter 12.

New wireless networking operating standards and products are frequently released. Although I advise against updating just for the heck of it, there will come a time that newly available products not around when you built your original wireless network will improve your network efficiency, speed and security. Chapter 13 covered how to stay in the loop with new products, and then how to efficiently manage any wireless network upgrades you choose to undertake.

Finally, Chapter 14 covered the exciting world of wireless Internet broadband access, and how to hook up your wireless LAN and WAN to the Web. In the world of communications, speed matters.

WHAT'S AHEAD

In the months and years ahead, wireless networking communications will become even faster and easier than now. In making this prediction, many wireless networking experts compare these trends to "Moore's Law." First proposed in 1965 by Intel Corp. cofounder Gordon Moore, Moore's Law now holds that the number of computer chips per square inch on integrated circuits will double every 18 months for the foreseeable future. Many experts think that because computer chips are also in the radio-like devices that power wireless networks, Moore's Law applies there, too.

Technology, of course, cannot thrive without market demand. Here, the progress of wireless networking seems to be unstoppable. Here are a few trends that prove my point:

- In September 2002, Morgan Stanley interviewed 225 chief information officers (CIOs) at companies in the United States. Of that number, 32 percent said they had already deployed a wireless network. An additional 24 percent were considering deployment.

- In the same survey, wireless network deployments ranked fifth in the CIO's list of deployment priorities for 2003. In the previous survey, the priority ranked seventeenth.

- Approximately 90 percent of the nation's universities and colleges used wireless LANs in 2002 compared to 50 percent the previous year. The source was research firm In-Stat/MDR.

- Gartner, Inc., a leading technology research company, estimates that within four years, 90 percent of all laptops in use at corporations will be Wi-Fi-enabled. As recently as the end of 2001, that number was only 20 percent.

This trend will receive a significant boost as a new generation of notebook computers with built-in Wi-Fi Internet access capabilities roll out in 2003 and beyond. Several laptop computers from Gateway, IBM, Toshiba (see Figure 15-1) and others will feature Centrino

Figure 15-1. Powered by Intel's Centrino Mobile Technology, the Toshiba Satellite Pro M15-S405 is one of the first notebook computers with built-in Wi-Fi Internet access capability.

Mobile Technology, a powerful new series of chips from leading chip-maker, Intel.

While the most common wireless network speed is 11 megabits per second, networking products manufacturer D-Link Systems has been marketing their AirPlus Access point and Airplus PCMCIA card for laptops with a communication speed of 22 megabits per second. This speed should increase further in the next year or so as the IEEE 802.11g standard, which calls for 54 megabits per second, is formally adopted and wireless network equipment manufacturers rush products to market capable of supporting these speeds.

The wireless networking revolution is here!

WIRELESS NETWORK ONLINE RESOURCES

While the information in this book is timely, the field of wireless networking is a dynamic one, constantly evolving with new products, solutions, and technical standards. This forward momentum is a good reason for you to familiarize yourself with on-line resources where you can obtain the very latest information about wireless personal area networks (PANs), local area networks (LANs), and wide area networks (WANs). There are resources where you can look for products, read reviews, line up your return-on-investment projections with case histories, and even discuss wireless network implementations with peers who have experience in this area.

The following list of wireless network on-line resources encompasses the topics discussed in this book. Because many of these resources discuss multiple topics covered in different chapters of this book, I have chosen to alphabetize the listings rather than break them down by relevance to specific book chapters.

Because of frequent product updates, as well as my reluctance to recommend specific products over competing ones, I also avoided sites offered by specific vendors.

Here, then, is a list of useful on-line wireless networking resources:

802.11Hotspots.com: A directory of Wi-Fi Internet access hot spots where you use your laptop to log on to the Internet at high speeds. The directory is searchable by city and state. *http://www.80211hotspots.com*

802.11Planet: This Web site posts the latest news about new wireless network products, technological advances, and regulatory issues. White papers with successful wireless network deployment case histories are also available. *http://www.80211-planet.com*

Airweb.ca: If you are traveling in Canada, this site will help you find a Wi-Fi hot spot where you will be able to use your wireless local area network (LAN)-enabled laptop computer. *http://www.airweb.ca/locations.html*

Bluetooth: The official Web site for the Bluetooth short-range wireless connectivity standard. On the site, you will find a search engine where you will be able to look for Bluetooth-enabled products and equipment. You will be able to reach the product search page directly at *http://www.bluetooth.com/tech/products.asp. http://www.bluetooth.com*

Bluetooth Weblog: Frequent news updates on Bluetooth technology and companies. The site's minders regularly look for Bluetooth articles from all over the Web, and post links to those articles here. *http://www.bluetooth.weblogs.com*

BoingoWireless: One of many high-speed Wi-Fi Internet access providers. The company offers a national network of several thousand wireless Internet "hot spots" where you can obtain access to the Internet over a Wi-Fi connection. Boingo also offers hot spot access software that is able to sense when you and your laptop are in range of a public wireless network. *http://www.boingo.com*

CNET.Com Network & Wireless: News and reviews of wireless and wired network products and solutions. *http://www. computers.cnet.com/hardware/O-1037.html?tag=quick*

High Performance Wireless Research and Education Network (HPWREN): A useful case study of a wireless wide area network deployment in San Diego, California. Many wireless wide area networks have been built for the purposes of research and educational communications. *http://www.hpwren.ucsd.edu*

Home RF News and Discussion Group: A forum for users of Home RF, a wireless networking standard for equipment in homes. Home RF uses the Shared Wireless Access Protocol (SWAP) specification, but has been losing momentum to Bluetooth as a wireless personal area network solution. *http://www.homerf.org*

Institute of Electrical and Electronics Engineers Standards Wireless Zone: Technical information about current and emerging technical standards for wireless personal, local, and wide area networks. *http://www.standards.ieee.org/wireless/*

ITtoolbox Wireless: News and on-line discussion groups for wireless network users, decision-makers, and developers. *http://www. Wireless.ITtoolbox.com*

Network Computing Magazine Mobile and Wireless Technology Guide: Frequently updated site offers news, product reviews, and buyer's guides for all types of wireless networks. *http://www.nwc. com/core/core3.html*

Palowireless Wireless Resource Center: Links to white papers and news updates about various wireless networking technologies. Subject areas are listed on the site's home page, and specific resources are a couple of clicks away at most. *http://www.palowireless.com*

Wi-Fi Alliance: Basic information about how Wi-Fi works, plus a search function where you can look for Wi-Fi enabled

Access Points, cards, gateways, and USB devices.
http://www.wi-fi.org

Wireless LAN Alliance: The site is the on-line presence of a consortium of wireless LAN equipment and service vendors. Here you will find white papers on wireless network inter-operability, security, and advanced technologies, as well as objective examinations of real-world Return On Investment (ROI) scenarios for building a wireless network. On *http://www.wlana.org/memb/index.htm,* you will find links to wireless LAN product pages for dozens of Wireless LAN equipment vendors. *http://www.wlana.org*

Wireless LAN Discussion Group: News and user discussions about wireless LAN deployment issues and technologies. *http://www. groups.yahoo.com/group.wirelesslan/*

WIRELESS NETWORKING GLOSSARY

As in any industry or profession, the world of wireless networking has its own "alphabet soup," its own jargon. Yet to some it may seem that wireless networking has more jargon than most other technology segments.

If this assertion is true, it is largely because wireless networking involves a mix of complex technologies, procedures, platforms, and standards that are not easily explainable in "plain" language. This leads to a forest of complex names that do not easily roll off the tongue—extended service set identification, point-to-point protocol over Ethernet, RC4 encryption algorithm. Mercifully, these procedures are sometimes initialized. Still, all this initialization is liable to produce a bit of head scratching.

This Wireless Networking Glossary is intended to explain the most common terms you will hear as you read and learn about this growing fieldand in applications that touch on related topics such as wired networking and wired and wireless network security. It is my hope that you will check this resource often, and also my expectation that doing so will help you through the jargon that this vital and growing technology has spawned.

2G   Refers to the "second generation" of mobile cellular communications. Unlike 1G, which was used mostly for voice communications, 2G incorporates a variety of digital voice and data capabilities. The most common of these data functions includes text-based messages, which cell phone service providers compose on their handset and send wirelessly from one cellular phone to another.

3DES (Triple Data Encryption Standard)   Enables secure text-based messages to be sent over the Internet or private communications networks. 3DES breaks up outgoing text into small 64-bit segments before sending them. In English a typical letter of the alphabet has seven or eight "bits." These bits are coded with "keys," tiny amounts of data that are intelligible only to the recipient. Although the earliest data encryption standards used keys with 56-bit segments, 3DES uses either 112- or 168-bit segments. Because the secure keys are larger in 3DES, they are that much harder to intercept. The trade-off is that data protected with 3DES takes slightly longer to decrypt, or "read," at the receiving end of the transmission.

3G   Refers to the "third generation" of mobile cellular communications. Whereas 1G was designed for cellular phone voice conversations, and 2G added the additional capability of short text message support, 3G supports high-speed multimedia data and voice transmissions. Optimal 3G systems, currently being constructed and introduced in North America, are intended to provide users with the ability to send a wireless transmission over the nearest available network, such as cellular or satellite equipment. 3G allows for communications of up to 144 kilobits per second of data (about three times faster than the fastest dial-up modems) from mobile locations and up to 2 megabits per second of data (slightly faster than the average transmission rate of high-speed cable modems) from fixed (land-based) locations.

5G   Now more theoretical than real, 5G refers to the "fifth generation" of mobile cellular communications. As envisioned, 5G devices would include, but not be limited to, "cognitive radio cell phones" that could recognize data and voice transmissions across multiple transmission standards and then reprogram themselves to send and receive these transmissions at high speeds. Such devices, at least in theory, would be capable of transmission-related tasks that now require separate devices, such as cell phones and pagers that use different transmission techniques.

64-bit key   A system of digits hidden, or encrypted, in a secure data transmission. In the most common method, outgoing text is broken up into small 64-bit segments before being sent. In English a typical letter of the alphabet has seven or eight "bits." These bits are coded with "keys," tiny amounts of data intelligible only to the recipient. In some cases the recipient would use a Web browser to "open" the file. Some data transmission standards have used keys with 56-bit segments.

802.11   A family of technical standards for data communication networks. Introduced in 1997 by the Institute of Electrical and Electronics Engineers, 802.11 now includes the 802.11 a, 802.11b, and the new 802.11g standards for wireless local area networks.

802.11a   Part of the 802.11 family of technical standards for wireless data communication networks, 802.11a theoretically is capable of supporting a maximum data rate of 54 megabits per second over wide, 5 GHz transmission channels. Proponents of 802.11a say that realistically, in high-volume environments such as offices, speeds of 20 to 25 megabits per second are far more common. That speed is still more than ten times as fast as high-rate T1 wired phone lines used to connect networks in many offices. Generally, the faster the speed, the shorter the transmission range. The effective maximum range of 802.11a transmissions spans 75 to 150 feet.

802.11b   Currently the most common technical standard for wireless local area networks, 802.11b is also known as "Wi-Fi." These networks have traditionally operated at a maximum speed of 11 megabits per second over 2.4 GHz transmission channels.

That maximum speed is being upgraded to 54 megabits per second. Even though the speed can be half that in some conditions, the rate is still several times as fast as high-rate T1 wired phone lines used to connect networks in many offices. As with 802.11a, generally, the faster the speed of the transmission, the shorter the transmission range. The effective maximum range of 802.11b transmissions reach from 75 to 150 feet. Currently, 802.11b is the most common standard and the one most often found in newly sold notebook computers. It is used for wireless network transmission in offices, as well as in coffee shops and airports, where wireless Internet access is provided by wireless Internet service providers in locations popularly known as "hot spots." A Wi-Fi enabled notebook computer would be used to access the Internet at a hot spot.

802.11g   Ratified in June 2003, 802.11g is the newest technical standard for wireless networks. The standards call for data transmission to be possible at speeds from 11 to 54 megabits per second. Although 802.11a also offers such speeds, its use of 5 GHz transmission channels makes its signals unintelligible to 802.11b, or Wi-Fi, enabled devices configured to work on the 2.4 GHz. Proponents of 802.11g note that because such transmissions will use the already commonplace 2.4 GHz rate, wireless 802.11g transmissions will be intelligible to a greater range of devices than 802.11a. In other words, 802.11g will provide for faster wireless networking transmissions using the same data channels now in widespread use. By early in 2004 a large number of 802.11g-compatible products are to hit the marketplace.

802.11n   First proposed in June, 2003, 802.11n is a possible future technical standard for Wireless Area Networks. The standard, which boosts the theoretical maximum speed of wireless Local Area Networks to at least 100 megabits per second, is under preliminary study by the Institute of Electrical and Electronics Engineers.

802.15   An Institute of Electrical and Electronics Engineers standard for wireless personal area networks that use the Bluetooth technology. The standard specifies how digital cellular phones, printers, computers, and personal digital assistants interconnect with each other and with other computers or computing-related devices. IEEE currently is researching several prospective future versions of 802.15. Groups are examining methods for reducing interference between Bluetooth networks and 802.11 wireless networksand examining the feasibility of faster Bluetooth wireless personal area networks than the 720 Kbps (kilobits per second) speeds currently available.

802.16   The 802.16 standards are for high-speed wireless metropolitan area networks, or wireless MANs. These are wireless wide area networks that, as might be indicated by name, cover a city or metropolitan area. This is another IEEE standard, the theoretical basis of which was approved in 2001. Currently an IEEE working group is researching ways to apply the standard, secure deployment of 10 to 66 GHz (gigahertz) transmission channel wireless wide area networks as an economical method of high-speed connections to public networks, such as phone lines. The family of enhanced 802.16 standards receiving or expecting approval in 2003 was 802.16a, 802.16.2a, 802.16c, 802.16.1, 802.16.2, 802.16.3, 802.16d, and 802.16e. All these elements relate to specific performance attributes of wireless MANs.

Access Point   These devices are base stations, often in the center of a group of computing and communication devices in a wireless local area network (WLAN). Most access points are stand-alone devices that plug into an Ethernet hub or server and then connect to the office's wired local area network. Typical range for an access point is around 150 feet but can be as little as half that when obstacles such as brick walls interfere with direct wireless transmission. As a user walks around a WLAN-enabled office with a notebook computer, the notebook computer is "handed off" from one access point to the next.

ACL (Access Control List)   In an office environment such lists might contain data files that indicate which users have permission to access wireless or wired networks or the specific devices on a wireless or a wired network.

ADC (Automated Data Collection)   A family of technologies used by data-collection devices and tools such as smart cards and barcode scanners. In retail, warehouse, and factory environments ADC-enabled bar code scanners can read information about products and then send it over wireless local area networks to a central inventory control database in the main office. ADC should not be confused with "analog to digital converter," which involves the use of specialized equipment to change analog signals (such as the human voice) to digital signals.

Add/Edit Configuration Profile   Most software used to set up a notebook computer or other device that works with an access point includes an add/edit configuration profile. Typically, this is a box where, among other steps, you enter the name of your wireless networking card, the name of your access point, and specific connection information.

Ad-Hoc Mode   A method of connecting two wireless-enabled devices to work directly with, and only with, each other. These devices send signals intended exclusively for the other device. This method is also known as peer-to-peer or independent basic server set. In this mode an access point is not necessary.

AES (Advanced Encryption Standard)   This standard uses 128-, 192- and 256-bit keys. In English a typical letter of the alphabet has seven or eight "bits." These bits are coded with "keys," tiny amounts of data that are intelligible only to the recipient. Whereas the earliest data encryption standards used keys with 56-bit segments, and 3DES uses either 112 or 168-bit segments, AES's 256-key limit provides extra levels of data protection. Because the secure keys are larger than even 3DES, they are that much more difficult to intercept. The trade-off is that data protected with AES takes slightly longer to decrypt, or "read," at the receiving end of the transmission.

Air Sniffer   In the wireless world this term has two meanings.

Air sniffers are software tools that can be installed on wireless local area networks or on devices connected to such networks to determine whether unauthorized users are attempting to gain access to the network. The term, more commonly shortened to "Sniffer," is also used to describe software that runs on a Wi-Fi enabled notebook computer and that can detect the presence of one or more Wi-Fi "hot spots" in the immediate area.

Algorithm   A mathematical formula or the steps in a computer program intended to achieve a stated result.

Authentication   Any of several systems or methods for verifying an electronic message or a user attempting to log on to a network, including a wireless network. Authentication can include encryption of messages, digital certificates to ensure that the person who is sending the message actually is that individual, implementation of passwords necessary to log on and retrieve messages and other data, or a combination of some or all of these methods.

Base Station   Apple Computer's term for an access point. As with access points, Apple Computer's base stations are often in the center of a group of computing and communication devices in a wireless local area network (WLAN). Most access points are stand-alone devices that plug into an Ethernet hub or server and then connect to the office's wired local area network. Typical range for an access point is around 150 feet but can be as little as half that when obstacles such as brick walls interfere with direct wireless transmission. As a user walks around a WLAN-enabled office with a notebook computer, the notebook computer will be "handed off" from one access point to the next.

Bluetooth   Established in 1998 by a consortium of mobile device manufacturers, Bluetooth is a wireless personal area networking standard for transmission of voice and data between desktop devices, such as computers, printers, and scanners, and mobile communications equipment such as cell phones and personal digital assistants. Bluetooth offers data transfer as fast as 720 Kbps within a range of around 33 feet, or about 10 meters.

The technology uses radio waves that can go through walls and other nonmetal materials. Bluetooth uses a type of transmission technique called spread spectrum, which calls for 1600 signal changes per second. The name of Bluetooth comes from a tenth century Danish king.

Bluetooth Special Interest Group   Also known as Bluetooth SIG, this Overland Park, Kansas-based entity is an association of computing, telecommunications, and networking supply companies charged with creating short-range wireless communication solutions for mobile products. Key corporate members of the organization include 3Com, Agere, Ericsson, IBM, Intel, Microsoft, Motorola, Nokia, and Toshiba.

Bridge   In the wireless as well as the wired networking world, this refers to any type of device that connects two networks together via an ability to switch signals between one network and another. Ethernet is the most common wired networking bridge technology.

Category 5 Cabling   Also known as CAT 5, this is a type of cabling that, among other uses, can connect wireless networks to wired networks, either directly or through access points. Newer types of Category 5 cabling known as Category 5 Enhanced can support transfers via gigabit Ethernet, which is rated for up to 100 million bits (the digital equivalent of around 2 million words) per second. These cabling standards are authored and approved by the Telecommunications Industry Association, a trade group of firms that provide communications and information technology products and services.

Category 6 Cabling   Also known as CAT 6, Category 6 cabling also offers gigabit Ethernet data transfers, but is said to offer a richer, less interference-prone connection than Category 5 Cabling. Recently released, Category 6 cabling is being positioned by its approval body, the Telecommunications Industry Association, as having the potential to handle multigigabit applications. These capabilities would be a marked improvement from Category 5 Enhanced cabling, which can support gigabit Ethernet data transfers of up to 100 million bits per second.

Cellular Digital Packet Data (CDPD)   A digital wireless standard mainly used to boost the data transmission speeds of older analog cellular phone networks. In the late 1990s services using cellular digital packet data technology were used to tie mobile devices, such as notebook computers, to the Internet. Because existing cellular networks are used, CDPD has been seen as a low-expense way of sending short text and e-mail messages through existing cell phone networks.

Central Processing Unit (CPU)   The processing section of a desktop or notebook computer. The CPU consists of a control unit and an arithmetic logic unit circuit. The control unit is hardware that performs the transfer of data from a computer's memory to a disk or to a computer monitor where it will be displayed. The arithmetic logic unit circuit facilitates the calculating and comparing necessary for processing commands issued to the computer from a user.

Centrino   Introduced by Intel in 2003, Centrino is a set of chips for mobile computers that preconfigures these devices for Wi-Fi wireless networking and Internet access. As this book went to press, computer manufacturers with Centrino products available or in the short-term pipeline included Acer, Alienware, ChemUSA, Dell, Equus, Fujitsu, Gateway, IBM, MDG, Motion Computing, Panasonic, Sony, Systemax, Toshiba and ZT Group.

Client Manager Software   Tools or applications that when used in wireless networks can monitor and rate the speed and transmission accuracy of those networks. In just one example, the ORiNOCO Client Manager utility indicates the wireless transmission signal level, noise level, and number of messages transferred at various speeds. Based in part on this information, this utility "grades" the overall connection quality.

Connect on Demand   In some wireless networking software utilities, a setting that enables a network connection immediately on a user action to do so. If connect on demand is not enabled, there may be a delay of several seconds before the connection is made.

Data Packet   A section, or "frame," of data included as part of a message sent over a wireless or wired network. A packet is a block of data ranging from 64 bytes (about the equivalent of ten words of text) to up to 1,518 bytes for some high-speed wireless network transmissions over wireless local area networks.

Denial of Service Attack   When a Web site or e-mailbox is maliciously flooded with too many "requests" for it to respond to, it will either slow down to handle the requests or temporarily break down as if weary from the overload. Denial of service attacks are usually committed by hackers, often those with an axe to grind against the company or organization whose Web site they choose to affect. In some cases these attacks are committed by multiple computers, each working in tandem with the others to send out bogus page or transaction requests to the targeted Web site. The most common of these attacks are called "buffer attacks." These actions involve either rigging computers to send out more packets (sections of data) than the site's computers can handle at any one given time or e-mail attachments with extremely long file names, which the site's e-mailboxes will struggle to open. No matter what the attack method, the consequences are painful for the targeted site. If the site is in the dot-com domain, for example, important customer contact information can be lost.

DES (Data Encryption Standard)   A generic term for a method of securing data traveling across wired or wireless networks. Data is encrypted with a series of digits, or a "key." For every 64-bit block of text (equivalent to around ten words), a 56-bit "key" is added. That key can only be opened by the intended recipient. Often this process involves a Web browser or e-mail program armed with the security tools that enable it to "recognize" that the message or form filled out on a Web page and then sent out over the Internet is intended for that recipient and that recipient alone.

DHCP (Dynamic Host Configuration Protocol)   This is software that automatically assigns numerical addresses to computer terminals the users of which are logging on to a wired or wireless network. Your specific Internet connection should have one of these numerical addresses for the duration of the time you use your current machine to access the Internet with your current service provider. This address is called an IP (Internet protocol) address. In an office setting each computer equipped for Internet connectivity must also have a unique IP address. When an organization sets up its computer users with a connection to the Internet, each device must receive its own IP address. DHCP automates the process. If it were not for DHCP, an IP address would have to be entered manually and reassigned if the computer were moved to another location on the network. Given that such portability is a big advantage of wireless networking, having to enter a new IP address manually would plainly be counterintuitive.

Diag LED   This is short for diagnostic light emitting diode, a display on a networking device such as a router. Depending on the router manufacturer, the Diag LED may either stay on rather than switch off or "blink" a certain color when the network is encountering transmission or reception problems.

DSL (Digital Subscriber Line)   This is a type of fast Internet access technology most commonly delivered over telephone lines. Because DSL uses higher frequencies than the voice band, it can send and deliver data at a faster rate. Often this capability is accomplished by a POTS (plain old telephone service) splitter, which a phone company technician installs at the customer's premises to separate the voice line you are talking on from the data line that is being set up. Newer types of DSL services forego splitters, using low-pass filters to separate the voice and data traffic. Typical connection speeds range from 1.544 Mbps to 512 Kbps for data sent by a corporate user to an individual subscriber and about 128 Kbps for the transmission the user sends back.

EDI (Electronic Data Interchange)   A technology in which product orders, order confirmations, and invoices are sent between suppliers and customers. This technology predates widespread use of secure Web-based electronic commerce. As electronic commerce took off, EDI was in danger of being eclipsed, but in the last couple of years improvements in the way Web pages are encoded have provided at least some hope that EDI will be revived on Web-based platforms and connections.

Encryption   Conversion of data sent over a network into a form that is unintelligible to all users except its intended recipient. This task is done by the random insertion of numerical digits, or "keys," into the outgoing message or data. A Web browser, e-mail program, Web-enabled cell phone, or Internet-capable personal digital assistant has the necessary tools to convert the data or message back to its original form, in which it can be read by the recipient.

ESSID (Extended Service Set Identification)   In wireless networks a setting or series of settings that define the computing and communications devices authorized to work with access points on the network.

Ethernet   A series of technical standards for physical links between wired and wireless local area networks or within components of a wired local area network.

FCC (Federal Communications Commission)   A U.S. Government agency charged with regulating interstate and international communications by radio, television, wire, satellite, and cable. According to the agency its Wireless Communications Bureau "oversees cellular and PCS phones, pagers and two-way radios. This Bureau also regulates the use of radio spectrum to fulfill the communications needs of businesses, local and state governments, public safety service providers, aircraft and ship operators, and individuals."

Full-Duplex   A type of data transmission scheme used in networked computers or related devices. On a wireless or wired network equipped with full-duplex data transmission capabilities, data can be sent and received in both directions at the same time. For example, a wireless network with two computers has the capability of receiving data on one computer as another computer sends data out.

Gigahertz   One billion cycles per second, a measure of the changes over one second in the type of transmission used by some communications devices and their associated wired or wireless networks. Most often abbreviated as GHz. The term "Hertz" itself is named after German physicist Heinrich Hertz.

Half-Duplex   A type of data transmission scheme used in networked computers or related devices. On a wireless or wired network equipped with half-duplex data transmission settings or capabilities, data cannot be sent and received in both directions at the same time. For example, a wireless network with two computers must complete the process of receiving data before the computers on the network can send data out.

Handshaking   When a sending and receiving station on a network or a connection "recognize" each other, as well as the specific data transmission information that will be used by both stations (such as a wireless modem and an online service) each station sends out an electronic signal called a "handshake." Colloquially expressed, the handshaking "parties" are saying, "hello there, I recognize you, so let's talk."

Help Desk   A customer service facility set up by a company or organization for fielding requests from users or account holders. In recent years a number of help desk functions have been automated by answers accessible via a series of phone buttons pressed by the caller. In the online world, help desk functions increasingly are being handled by software that parses customer requests for words that might indicate the nature of the problem the customer is calling about, sending an electronic inquiry to a company database where suggestions for solving the problem can be found, and then sending a customized Web page to the end-user with information containing those suggestions.

HomeRF (Home Radio Frequency)   A type of wireless networking transmission technology that facilitates communication between wireless and wired devices. Derived from an old European standard for cordless telephones, HomeRF has unsuccessfully warded off competition from the newer and far more widespread 802.11 (Wi-Fi) set of standards. In this decade HomeRF's lack of traction in the market has been so acute that the standard's developing body, the HomeRF Working Group, disbanded in 2003.

Host Control Interface   Also known as HCI, this is a command interface that defines the interchange between various infrastructure levels on Bluetooth-enabled wireless personal area networks.

Hot Spot   A geographical region or location within the service boundary of a wireless Internet service provider (WISP). At such locations users with Wi-Fi equipped notebook computers can log on to the Internet through WISPs. Some WISPs require paid subscriptions for wireless Internet access, whereas others provide such access for free. Intel, whose Wi-Fi access-enabling Centrino computer chip debuted in 2003, now provides a searchable directory of hot spots. The Web address for this resource is http://www.intel.com/products/mobiletechnology/hotspots/finder.htm.

Infrastructure Mode   In this mode wireless or wired computing or communications devices associated with a wireless or wired network communicate with each other through an access point device. This method differs from ad-hoc mode, in which two devices communicate directly with one another.

InstallShield Wizard   A utility used by software developers to enable automatic installation of programs that users download from their sites or third-party services. The product is included with the software and does not require setup on end-users' PCs or notebook computers. Manufacturer is InstallShield Software Corporation, Schaumberg, Illinois.

Institute of Electrical and Electronic Engineers (IEEE)   This group of more than 380,000 members researches, drafts, and approves technical standards for wireless networks as well as a whole host of other technologies and applications. Consistently reviewed and periodically updated, the set of 802 wireless network standards is an ongoing enterprise of the IEEE. More information can be found on the IEE Web site at www.ieee.org.

Intrusion Detection System (IDS)   Software designed to detect illegal entrance or an attempt at same to a network or computer system. There are several types of IDSs, but most of them work by analyzing every attempt to access the network and then looking for anomalies in the nature of the access attempt that could point to unusual or even illegal intent. Most IDSs also point out errors in network settings that could leave the network vulnerable to attack.

IR (Infrared)   An invisible band of radiation used for wireless transmission between computing devices or in remote controls used in television and stereo equipment. Traditionally, IR has been regarded as a "line of sight" technology, which requires all the associated devices to be "visible" to each other. In wireless networksIR's key limitation is its general inability to pass through walls and many other solid services. In recent years a modest number of enhancements have been made to IR's line of sight limitations, but these improvements are generally regarded as not substantial enough to make IR a highly efficient solution for most wireless networks.

IrDA (Infrared Data Association   A technical standard that allows for wireless transmission between computing devices or in remote controls used in conjunction with television and stereo equipment. Your trusty TV remote control uses IrDA.

Keep Alive Option   This colorfully named capability is actually a wired or wireless network operation that works with network servers or access points to check the network connection for activity at varied intervals. When the Keep Alive Option is enabled, messages are sent from the controlling device to the various types of equipment on the network. The equipment is then supposed to acknowledge the message in a type of "hello, I am here" fashion. If the controlling device does not detect such messages of acknowledgments from the networked devices, and no other activity is being initiated, the controlling device generally considers the network "down."

Kilohertz   One thousand cycles per second, a measure of the changes over one second in the type of transmission used by some communications devices and their associated wired or wireless networks. Most often abbreviated as KHz. The term "Hertz" itself is named after German physicist Heinrich Hertz.

L2CAP (Logical Link Control and Adaptation Protocol)   A set of highly technical specifications for the efficient sending and receiving of data transmission over Bluetooth-enabled wireless personal area networks.

Link Controller   A hardware device that manages data traffic across local area networks and other data communications networks.

Link Manager Software   Utility that manages the data messages and signals sent across various points on local area networks.

Local Area Network   Also known as a "LAN," a network of computers, computing devices, and associated communications hardware connected together in a given space, such as a portion of an office floor. Local area networks may be wired and use cables to communicate; wireless, using an 802.11 signal connection; or a combination of both.

Logical Link Control   In wireless local area networks, a communications layer that identifies specific communications protocols to be used and then assigns sequence numbers to packets of data traveling across the network. This sequencing helps assure that these sections of data being sent arrive at the reception point in the order intended.

Media Access Control   A communications layer in wireless local area networks that regulates the sharing of access to the network among the computers and other devices associated with it.

Man in the Middle Attack   An Internet security violation in which a third party intercepts and modifies data messages between a sender and a receiver without the knowledge of either party. Secure Web-based transactions using various encryption key controls greatly reduce the risk of such attacks.

Master Switch   In computer networking, a device with a switch that controls the other devices on the network and participates in the particular transmission or user session. The devices that are being controlled are called "slaves"

Max Idle Time   A network management software setting that specifies how long a wired or wireless networking session can remain inactive before the connection self-terminates. In most cases the session is reactivated when a user with a computer connected to the network initiates mouse or keyboard activity. Most network management software offers settings that can disable the idle timer used to regulate the max idle time.

Microcells   This term has two meanings. In wireless networks microcells are small, usually set-off spaces where a number of wireless-enabled devices can communicate. Cellular phone companies also use "microcell" to define geographically consolidated service areas where cell traffic is high. Cell phone service providers build microcells when standard-area cells may run the risk of too much demand for an individual cell phone tower to handle. Incidentally, cell phone towers often handle the hand-off of traffic between points on a wireless wide area network.

NAT Address   NAT is short for network address translation, which occurs when an Internet protocol (IP) address used within one address is translated into another IP address. Use one set of IP addresses for internal traffic and a second set of addresses for external traffic. A NAT box located where the LAN meets the Internet makes all necessary IP address translations. NAT serves two main purposes: It provides a type of firewall by hiding internal IP addresses, and it enables a company to use more than one internal IP address. This is especially helpful for authorized Intranet as well as Internet connectivity from various points on a wireless local area network.

Network Analyzer   A family of software and hardware products that monitors the performance of local area networks and can identify transmission and other problems that may exist. Some advanced network analyzers can recognize, troubleshoot, and even recommend solutions for fixing such problems as delayed or unintentionally refused connections.

Network Topology Map   An actual map of a wireless or wired network, as it appears in the "real world." In a wireless local area network, for example, a network topology map would visually depict the distribution and location of various networked devices on an office floor. Several manufacturers offer software that can design such maps. Hewlett-Packard's HP Open View is one of the best-known network topology map authoring software utilities.

NIC (Network Interface Card)   A card or circuit board that plugs into a computer to enable connections to a wired or wireless network.

NIST (National Institute of Standards and Technology)   A unit of the U.S. Commerce Department. NIST's Wireless Communication Technologies Group helps develop industry consensus national and international standards for wireless communications; conducts basic and applied research in wireless communications to support testing, measurements, and standards; and develops tests and measurement methods for the U.S. wireless communications industry. NIST can be found on the Web at www.nist.gov.

Passthrough   In both wireless and wired networking, the setting of network management software to customize network access settings for a specific device or user on the network.

PBX (Private Branch Exchange)   A phone system within a company or office that allows users to share the same general telephone number, with extensions. This capability eliminates the considerable expense of separate outside phone numbers for each user.

PCMCIA Card   A card that inserts into a slot within a PC, usually a notebook computer. Such cards often enable the insertion of devices such as modems or Ethernet cards, intended for communication over networks or the Internet. PCMCIA stands for the Personal Computer Memory Card International Association, the trade group that devised the PCMCIA standard back in 1989. More information is available on the PCMCIA's Web site at www.pcmcia.org.

Peripheral Component Interconnect (PCI)   A system within a computer in which expansion slots for cards with new applications are placed closer together for faster operation with the computer itself. Known as PCI-X (for PCI Extended), the newest PCI designs allow data to move within a computer at speeds up to 1.06 gigabits per second. That speed is twice as fast as the earlier maximum 532 megabit per second performance of previous peripheral component interconnect technology. Plainly, the faster data and commands travel within a computer, the more efficient a computer works.

Peripheral Devices   Hardware that is neither a part of the core of a computer or a computer itself, but works in close association with a computer. A peripheral can be physically connected to a computer, such as a keyboard or monitor, or in the case of a printer, scanner, or fax machine, be close by and connected wirelessly or by means of cables.

Piconet   A network of at least two, but not more than eight, devices connected using Bluetooth technology. In a piconet, one device acts as the master, or controller. That device is usually the PC. The other devices, such as a personal digital assistant or a printer, are slaves, taking commands from the controller device. Another way to think of piconets is as visual representations or diagrams of the devices in and the design of a wireless personal area network.

PIN   This term has two meanings, neither of which have anything to do with the other. Most people associate the term with "personal identification number," which is used to obtain secure access to automated bank teller machines and even some Web sites. In the networking world, though, "pin" means a pronged interface at the point where a cable runs from a wired network or peripheral device associated with a computer to the computer itself.

Pocket PC   Microsoft's operating platform for personal digital assistants and digital cellular telephones. Pocket PC devices usually come with preinstalled, scaled-down versions of several popular Microsoft programs, such as Excel, Word, Outlook Express, and even Windows Media Player. An increasing number of Pocket PC devices are preinstalled to work with wireless local area networks and Bluetooth-enabled wireless personal area networks. A list of PocketPC devices is available on Microsoft's Web site at www.microsoft.com/mobile/pocketpc/hardware/americas.asp

PPPoE (Point-to-Point Protocol Over Ethernet)   A security standard for secure authentication of messages sent over a wireless Ethernet connection from a cable modem subscriber's computer on a local area network to a cable modem or digital subscriber line service provider's Internet traffic routing center. A process included with PPPoE can determine and verify the origination address of the remote device. When that information is authenticated, the session begins.

RC4 Encryption Algorithm   A technology that spawns a random stream of up to 256 bytes to generate up to 56 bits of security keys. These keys are then used to encrypt Internet commerce and messages. Devised in 1987 by RSA Data Security, Inc., RC4 is still in wide use but has largely been eclipsed by RC5, a somewhat more powerful but slower technology.

RF (Radio Frequency)   The range of electromagnetic frequencies above the audio range and below visible light. All transmissions are encompassed by this range, which is between 30 kHz and 300 GHz. This range is divided into nine sections called the spectrum. The frequency of a signal in any of the eight RF spectra is proportional to the length of the wave it sends out. The higher the frequency, the smaller the wave size will be. Some types of wireless communications use RF, such as cellular telephones, two-way radios, and satellite communications systems. When the length of the wave extends the electromagnetic frequency above the RF range, the signal is sometimes visible as either infrared or visible light. The majority of television remote control boxes and some cordless computer keyboards and mice use this range.

RFCOMM (Radio Frequency Communication)   A component of Bluetooth technology that supports its use in equipment connected to computers by means of serial ports at the back of the PC.

Rijndael   An Internet security algorithm recently selected by the National Institute of Standards and Technology as part of the next generation of encrypting online data and transmissions, making them secure. Rijndael uses a 128-bit, 192-bit, or 256-bit key to encrypt each successive 156-bit (the equivalent of around three words) of data. Rijndael is named after its inventors, Belgian cryptologists Vincent Rijmen and Joan Daemen.

RJ-45 (Register Jack-45)   A single-line jack and plug used in Ethernet as well as in a variety of digital-data-over-telephone applications and connections.

Router   A device on a computer or a network that sends, or "routes," successive packets of data toward their intended destinations. An example would be a handoff that would send a packet of data in an outbound e-mail from a computer on a local area network to another local area network or to a company e-mail server or firewall. Routers read the intended address in each group of data and then make the appropriate decision about where the data should go and the most efficient way for it to get there.

SDP (Service Discovery Protocol) A component in Bluetooth that identifies the type of technical request submitted by a user of a Bluetooth network and then clears the path for routing the request to the appropriate device.

Slave A device or set of devices in a wired or wireless network that takes its direction from a command device. In a wireless personal area network an example of a slave would be a printer or a computer controlled by the central, or "master," computer.

Smart Card A credit-card size plastic card containing a microchip loaded with encrypted data. Holding more information than the standard magnetic strips on the back of charge cards, this data often is personalized for an individual user or contains a stored cashed value for small purchases at stores and gas stations. Some new Wi-Fi enabled notebook computers, such as Hewlett-Packard's Compaq Evo N620c, contain smart card readers for access to and control of the deviceand for certain types of Internet commerce transactions.

SSID (Service Set Identifier) A set of characters that assigns a unique name to a wireless local area network (WLAN) or to a group of WLANs in a company or organization. This name allows devices normally associated with one WLAN to connect to another WLAN at the same company or organization. This is possible because even though the other WLAN is controlled through another access point, the SSID normally is the same.

TCP (Transmission Control Protocol) A set of rules for sending and receiving messages or Web pages over the Internet. TCP prepares data for this process by dividing it into packets for efficient transmission.

Terminal Emulation Software This software's most frequent uses are to make one computer monitor look like another or perform certain tasks without installing the task program on the user's machine. One common example is a type of terminal emulation that shows a plain-text only e-mail or Web page interface.

Triple-DES   An advanced data encryption standard that works by performing three successive encryption key-spawning operations. These keys are then added to the content that is being encrypted. The extra keys produced in this process make the encrypted content—such as an e-mail or response to a form on a Web page—much more difficult to intercept and crack than simpler DES methods.

Twofish   An alternate encryption standard for securing Internet content and electronic mail, Twofish was evaluated by the National Institute of Standards and Technology as a possible replacement for DES (data encryption standard) encryption. Although Twofish was not selected, the unpatented and free program has achieved significant popularity as an encryption standard for Smart Cards. More information, including a free download of the basic code for Twofish, is available on the Counterpane Internet Security, Inc. Web site at www.counterpane.com/twofish.html.

Universal Serial Bus   More commonly referred to as USB, this is an interface between a computer and any one of several types of add-on devices. In traditional USB deployment the user plugs a cable that comes with specific equipment (such as a digital camera or printer) into a port on a USB device. In turn, the USB device is plugged in to the computer. In the Wi-Fi world several manufacturers make USB adapters. The main function of these adapters is to connect a desktop or laptop to a wireless network. Usually these adapters include a standard USB cable, which connects to any available USB port on a laptop or desktop Windows-based PC.

vCard   An electronic business card that can be personalized with customized audio messages, photos, and company logos. vCards can be sent as e-mail or attached files over Wi-Fi or traditional land-based Internet connections.

Voice Over IP   A set of technical specifications for sending voice over the Internet rather than through traditional telephone circuits. These messages are divided into packets, just as data is.

Not all voice-over-IP applications enable users to hear the message over an Internet connection, but some Wi-Fi service providers can work with Internet telephony software or services to enable users to talk wirelessly over their wireless network-enabled notebook computers.

VPN (Virtual Private Network)   Usually, VPNs are a proprietary series of connections that use the Internet or existing phone networks but use routing arrangements known as "tunneling" to set the connections apart from standard Internet or general phone network traffic. VPNs are frequently utilized to enable wired and wireless mobile and remote users to establish connections from their notebook computers to their company or organization's internal local area networks.

Wide Area Network   A wired or wireless geographically dispersed communications network, such as a network that encompasses several buildings on a college campus or business locations within a given metropolitan area. Some wide area networks cover states or entire nations. Wide area networks that are restricted to a single metropolitan region are sometimes referred to as MANs, or metropolitan area networks.

Wi-Fi (Wireless Fidelity)   The popular brand name for wireless local area network. Many corporate users are embracing Wi-Fi as an economical, low-hassle alternative to wired local area networks. Additionally, Wi-Fi is catching on as a method for fast mobile Internet access by means of Wi-Fi enabled notebook computers and hot spots within range of wireless Internet service provider coverage areas. The Wi-Fi specification is synonymous with the 802.11b technical standard issued by the Institute of Electrical and Electronics Engineers. This standard calls for a theoretical maximum data speed of up to 11 megabits per second, but emerging standards and compatible equipment are poised to raise this theoretical limit to 54 megabits per second.

Wired Equivalent Privacy   A security protocol for wireless local area networks, wired equivalent privacy works by encrypting data transmitted over the wireless local area network

(WLAN). The backers of this protocol say this extra protection is necessary because radio waves transmitted over a WLAN in an office environment could, at least in theory, "leak out" of the office building and within range of an interception device. Although wired equivalent privacy's backers note that this method is not a substitute for encrypting data at the source, the overall effectiveness of wired equivalent privacy has been questioned by some experts.

Wired Network Jack   A receptacle for plugging a cable from a wireless local area network access point into a computer or similar device running a wired local area network.

Wireless LAN Association   A trade organization comprised of leading hardware, software, component, training, and wireless Internet access companies in the wireless local area networking industry. The Wireless LAN Association's Web site is located at www.wlana.org.

Wireless LAN Card   A card inserted into a notebook computer that equips the computer for wireless local area network and wireless Internet access. Many, if not most, new notebook computers come with wireless LAN cards already installed.

Wireless Local Area Network (WLAN)   A network that allows mobile users to connect to their wired local area networks or the Internet through a wireless connection. The family of standards for WLANs is collectively known as 802.11 and is administered by the Institute of Electrical and Electronics Engineers.

Wireless Personal Area Network   A networking technology that allows for transfer of data between several mobile devices and a PC within 33 feet of each other. Bluetooth is the most common type of wireless personal area network. One reason this technology is becoming popular is because it greatly reduces the need for unsightly wires and cables.

Wireless Wide Area Network (WWAN)   Networks that can encompass different areas within large office complexes or even within metropolitan areas. Unlike wireless local area networks, the coverage area for WWANs is usually measured in miles rather than feet. These networks use coverage cells (microcells) created by access points and similar to the cell phone system to extend the range of wireless connectivity.

WISP (Wireless Internet Service Provider)   A company or service that facilitates connection to the Internet via notebook computers and other mobile devices. Many WISPs offer subscription-based access at hot spots such as airports and coffee shops. Some leading WISPs are Boingo Wireless (www.boingo.com), T-Mobile (www.t-mobile.com), and Wayport (www.wayport.com). A searchable list of WISPs and Hot Spots is available on the 802.11 Planet Web site at www.80211hotspots.com.

A QUICK GUIDE TO WIRELESS NETWORK STANDARDS

In most technology industries where innovation is consistent, a series of technical standards exist.

The main reason for these standards in the wireless networking world is to guide product manufacturers and service providers to develop products and offerings that work together in a common framework. If these standards were not in place, competitive companies would form consortia to make products that would not work with those made by rivals. Significant confusion would result, which would inhibit acceptance of wireless networking among consumers and businesses.

Fortunately, standards do exist. The main standards bodies are the National Institute of Standards and Technology, (NIST), a unit of the U.S. Commerce Department; and the Institute of Electrical and Electronic Engineers, more commonly referred to as the IEEE. The IEEE has several working groups that research, propose, and approve these standards.

Additionally, the Wireless Ethernet Compatibility Alliance tests and certifies products manufactured for use on or with wireless local area networks. In the wireless personal area network sector substantial equipment testing and approval is conducted and granted by the Bluetooth Special Interest Group's PAN Working Group.

As a general rule, there is a time lag of between six months to a year between approval of wireless networking standards and widespread availability of wireless networking products and services compatible with that standard.

For our purposes, let us examine the three main families of technical standards applicable to wireless networking. These are 802.11, 802.15, and 802.16.

UNDERSTANDING THE 802.11 STANDARD

802.11 is a family of technical standards for wireless local area networks. Introduced in 1997 by the Institute of Electrical and Electronics Engineers, 802.11 now includes the 802.11a, 802.11b, and the new 802.11g standards.

The 802.11 standard's main established and developmental components are sometimes called Working Groups after the IEEE's name for groups under its aegis that develop these standards. The most important standards associated with these Working Groups include those discussed in the following paragraphs.

802.11a

Theoretically, the 802.11a standard is capable of supporting a maximum data rate of 54 megabits per second over wide 5 Ghz transmission channels. Proponents of 802.11a say that in high-volume environments such as offices speeds of 20 to 25 megabits per second are far more realistic an expectation. That speed is still more than ten times as fast as high-rate T1 wired phone lines used to connect networks in many offices. Generally, the faster the speed, the shorter the transmission range.

The effective maximum range of 802.11a transmissions span 75 to 150 feet.

802.11b

Currently the most common technical standard for wireless local area networks, 802.11b is also known as "Wi-Fi." These networks have traditionally operated at a maximum speed of 11 megabits per second over 2.4 GHz transmission channels. That maximum speed is being upgraded to 54 megabits per second. Even though the speed can be half that in some conditions, the rate is still several times as fast as high-rate T1 wired phone lines used to connect networks in many offices. As with 802.11a, the faster the speed of the transmission, the shorter the transmission range, generally. The effective maximum range of 802.11b transmissions is 75 to 150 feet. Currently, 802.11b is the most common standard and is becoming standard issue in newly sold notebook computers. It is used in for wireless network transmission in offices, as well as in coffee shops and airports, where wireless Internet access is provided by wireless Internet service providers in locations popularly known as "hot spots." A Wi-Fi enabled notebook computer would be used to access the Internet at a hot spot.

802.11g

Ratified in June 2003, 802.11g is the newest technical standard for wireless networks. The standards call for data transmission to be possible at speeds from 11 to 54 megabits per second. Although 802.11a also offers such speeds, its use of 5 GHz transmission channels makes its signals unintelligible to 802.11b, or Wi-Fi, enabled devices configured to work on the 2.4 GHz. Proponents of 802.11g note that because such transmissions use the already commonplace 2.4 GHz rate, wireless 802.11g transmissions will be intelligible to a greater range of devices than 802.11a. In other words, 802.11g will provide for faster wireless networking transmissions using the same data channels now in widespread use. By early in 2004 a large number of 802.11g-compatible products are to hit the marketplace.

ALL IN THE FAMILY:
OTHER 802.11 STANDARDS

Several other 802.11 standards have less direct relevance for most wireless network users, but deserve at least a brief mention. These include those discussed in the following paragraphs.

802.11d

This IEEE Working Group is developing standards for 802.11 wireless local area networking equipment for use in nations that have not approved the current major 802.11 standards.

802.11f

This IEEE Working Group is developing an interaccess point protocol, intended to make it easier for wireless devices to be universally used with access points made by different vendors.

802.11h

This IEEE Working Group is developing spectrum and power management solutions for 802.11a networks and equipment intended for European use.

The latest information on all IEEE 802.11 standards initiatives is available on the IEEE Web site at http://grouper.ieee.org/groups/802/11/.

802.11n

First proposed in June, 2003, 802.11n is a possible future technical standard for Wireless Area Networks. The standard, which boosts the theoretical maximum speed of wireless Local Area Networks to at least 100 megabits per second, is under preliminary study by the Institute of Electrical and Electronics Engineers.

UNDERSTANDING THE 802.15 STANDARD

The 802.15 standard is an Institute of Electrical and Electronics Engineers standard for wireless personal area networks that use the Bluetooth technology. The standard specifies how digital cellular phones, printers, computers, and personal digital assistants interconnect with each other and with other computers or computing-related devices. IEEE currently is researching several prospective future versions of 802.15. Groups are examining methods for reducing interference between Bluetooth networks and 802.11 wireless networksand examining the feasibility of faster Bluetooth wireless personal area networks than the 720 Kbps speeds currently available. The latest information on 802.15 standards research is available on the IEEE Web site at http://grouper.ieee.org/groups/802/15/.

UNDERSTANDING THE 802.16 STANDARD

The 802.16 standards are for high-speed wireless metropolitan area networks, or wireless MANs. These are wireless wide area networks that cover a city or metropolitan area. This is another IEEE standard, the theoretical basis of which was approved in 2001. Currently an IEEE working group is researching ways to apply the standard, secure deployment of 10 to 66 GHz transmission channel wireless wide area networks, as an economical method of high-speed connections to public networks such as phone lines.

The family of enhanced 802.16 standards receiving or expecting approval in 2003 is 802.16a; 802.16.2a; 802.16c; 802.16.1; 802.16.2; 802.16.3; 802.16d; and 802.16e. All these elements relate to specific performance attributes of wireless MANs.

INDEX